How to Start a Profitable Online Business from Home

The Ultimate Guide to Building a Thriving E-commerce Business, Affiliate Marketing Empire, or Freelancing Career Using SEO, Content Marketing, and Digital Advertising Strategies

The Fix It Guy

Copyright © 2024 by The Fix It Guy

All rights reserved. No part of this book may be reproduced in any form or by any electronic or mechanical means, including information storage and retrieval systems, without permission in writing from the publisher, except by a reviewer who may quote brief passages in a review.

Table of Contents

Introduction

Chapter 1: Discovering Your Passion and Choosing a Profitable Niche
- Identifying Your Skills, Interests, and Expertise
- Researching Market Demand and Competition
- Narrowing Down Your Niche and Validating Your Idea

Chapter 2: Understanding Different Online Business Models
- E-commerce: Building an Online Store
- Affiliate Marketing: Promoting Other People's Products
- Freelancing: Offering Your Services Online
- Digital Products: Creating and Selling Your Own Products
- Coaching and Consulting: Sharing Your Expertise

Chapter 3: Setting Up Your Online Business Foundation
- Choosing a Domain Name and Web Hosting
- Designing Your Website and Branding
- Essential Tools and Software for Running Your Business
- Legal Requirements and Business Registration

Chapter 4: Mastering Search Engine Optimization (SEO)
- Understanding How Search Engines Work
- Keyword Research and Analysis
- On-Page SEO: Optimizing Your Website's Content and Structure
- Off-Page SEO: Building Quality Backlinks and Improving Your Site's Authority

Chapter 5: Creating Compelling Content for Your Website
- Identifying Your Target Audience and Their Pain Points
- Developing a Content Strategy and Editorial Calendar
- Writing Engaging Blog Posts and Articles
- Incorporating Multimedia Content (Videos, Podcasts, Infographics)
- Repurposing and Updating Your Content

Chapter 6: Leveraging Social Media for Business Growth
- Choosing the Right Social Media Platforms for Your Business
- Creating a Social Media Strategy and Content Plan
- Growing Your Followers and Engagement
- Running Social Media Ads and Promotions
- Collaborating with Influencers and Other Businesses

Chapter 7: Implementing Effective Email Marketing Strategies
- Building Your Email List and Lead Magnets
- Segmenting Your Subscribers and Personalizing Your Emails
- Crafting Compelling Email Copy and Subject Lines
- Automating Your Email Campaigns and Sales Funnels

Chapter 8: Scaling Your Online Business and Increasing Revenue
- Diversifying Your Income Streams and Offerings
- Outsourcing and Building a Team
- Analyzing Your Metrics and Making Data-Driven Decisions
- Continuously Improving Your Products and Services

Chapter 9: Maintaining Work-Life Balance and Avoiding Burnout
- Setting Realistic Goals and Boundaries
- Prioritizing Self-Care and Mental Health
- Automating and Streamlining Your Business Processes
- The Importance of Continuous Learning and Personal Development

Conclusion
- Recap of Key Takeaways and Action Steps
- The Future of Online Business and Emerging Trends
- Encouragement and Motivation for the Reader's Journey Ahead

Introduction

Hey there, future online business rockstar!

Imagine waking up every morning, sipping your favorite coffee, and sitting down at your computer to work on your very own online business. No more commuting, no more bosses breathing down your neck, and no more trading your precious time for a measly paycheck. Sounds like a dream come true, right?

Well, I'm here to tell you that this dream can become your reality, and I'm living proof of it! Hi, I'm [Your Name], and I've built a thriving online business from the comfort of my own home. It wasn't always easy, and I had my fair share of doubts and setbacks along the way. But with the right strategies, mindset, and a whole lot of determination, I turned my passion into a profitable venture that has transformed my life in ways I never thought possible.

In this book, I'm going to share with you all the secrets, tips, and tactics that I've learned on my journey to online business success. Whether you're looking to start an e-commerce store, become a top-notch affiliate marketer, offer your freelance services, create digital products, or share your expertise through coaching and consulting, I've got you covered.

But here's the thing: starting an online business isn't just about making money (although that's definitely a huge perk!). It's about freedom, flexibility, and the ability to design a life that truly fulfills you. Imagine having the time and financial security to travel the world, pursue your hobbies, spend quality time with your loved ones, and make a positive impact in your community. That's the real power of building an online business from home.

Now, I know what you might be thinking: "But, I don't have any experience, I'm not tech-savvy, and I have no idea where to start!" Trust me, I've been there. When I first started out, I was overwhelmed, confused, and full of self-doubt. But I refused to let those fears hold me back, and I'm so glad I didn't. With the right guidance, tools, and support, anyone can build a successful online business, no matter their background or skill level.

So, if you're ready to take control of your financial future, escape the 9-to-5 grind, and turn your passions into profits, then this book is for you. I'll be your personal guide, cheerleader, and mentor every step of the way. Together, we'll dive into the nitty-gritty of choosing your niche, setting up your online presence, mastering search engine optimization, creating irresistible content, leveraging social media, and so much more.

But more than just teaching you the technical stuff, I'm going to share with you the mindset shifts, productivity hacks, and self-care practices that have been essential to my success. Because let's face it, building an online business can be a rollercoaster ride, and you need to be mentally and emotionally prepared for the ups and downs.

Chapter 1
Discovering Your Passion and Choosing a Profitable Niche

Identifying Your Skills, Interests, and Expertise

Hey there, aspiring online entrepreneur! Let's dive into the first and most crucial step of starting your online business journey: discovering your passion and choosing a profitable niche. This is where the magic happens, and you lay the foundation for your future success.

Identifying Your Skills, Interests, and Expertise

Before you start brainstorming niche ideas, it's essential to take a deep dive into your own skills, interests, and expertise. This self-reflection will help you identify areas where you can provide the most value to your target audience and build a business that truly aligns with your passions.

Let's break it down:

1. Skills
- What are you naturally good at? What comes easily to you?
- What skills have you developed through education, training, or experience?
- Examples: writing, graphic design, programming, social media marketing, etc.

2. Interests
- What topics do you enjoy learning about or discussing with others?
- What activities make you lose track of time because you're so engrossed in them?
- Examples: fitness, personal development, fashion, cooking, travel, etc.

3. Expertise
- What subjects do you have in-depth knowledge or experience in?
- What problems have you solved or challenges have you overcome in your life or career?
- Examples: managing finances, parenting, overcoming anxiety, learning a new language, etc.

Now, I want you to grab a pen and paper (or open up a fresh document on your computer) and start brainstorming. List out all of your skills, interests, and areas of expertise, no matter how big or small they may seem. Don't hold back – this is your chance to really explore what makes you unique and valuable.

Once you have your list, start looking for patterns and connections. Are there any themes that keep popping up? For example, maybe you're skilled at writing and have a deep interest in wellness, with expertise in yoga and meditation. That could be a powerful combination for a niche focused on mindfulness and self-care.

But don't just stop at one idea! Keep exploring different combinations and angles. You might be surprised at how many potential niches you have hidden within your own experiences and passions.

Remember, choosing a niche isn't just about finding something that you're good at or interested in – it's also about identifying a profitable market. In the next section, we'll dive into how to research market demand and competition to ensure that your niche has the potential to generate income and support your business goals.

But for now, focus on getting crystal clear on what makes you tick. Because when you build a business around your passions and strengths, not only will you be more motivated and fulfilled, but you'll also be able to provide incredible value to your target audience.

So, take your time with this process, and don't be afraid to explore, dream, and get creative. Your perfect niche is out there waiting for you – it's up to you to discover it!

Researching Market Demand and Competition

Alright, now that you've identified your skills, interests, and expertise, it's time to take the next step in choosing a profitable niche: researching market demand and competition. This is where you'll dig deep into the viability of your niche ideas and ensure that there's a hungry market of potential customers waiting for your offerings.

Let's break down the process:

1. Identify Your Target Audience
- Who are the people most likely to benefit from your skills, interests, and expertise?
- What are their demographics (age, gender, location, income level, etc.)?
- What are their pain points, challenges, and desires?
- Example: If your niche is mindfulness and self-care, your target audience might be stressed-out millennials seeking work-life balance and mental well-being.

2. Conduct Keyword Research
- Use tools like Google Keyword Planner, SEMrush, or Ahrefs to research keywords related to your niche.
- Look for keywords with high search volume and low competition.
- Identify long-tail keywords that indicate specific problems or desires within your niche.
- Example: For the mindfulness and self-care niche, keywords might include "stress reduction techniques," "mindfulness meditation for beginners," or "self-care routine ideas."

3. Analyze Competitor Websites
- Search for websites, blogs, and online businesses already serving your target audience in your chosen niche.
- Analyze their content, offerings, branding, and marketing strategies.
- Look for gaps in the market or areas where you could differentiate yourself and provide unique value.
- Example: In the mindfulness and self-care niche, you might find that most competitors focus on yoga and meditation, but there's a gap in the market for self-care products or coaching services.

4. Engage with Your Target Audience
- Join online communities, forums, and social media groups where your target audience hangs out.
- Observe their conversations, questions, and challenges to gain insight into their needs and desires.
- Engage in discussions and offer helpful advice or resources to build trust and credibility.
- Example: For the mindfulness and self-care niche, you might join Facebook groups for stressed-out professionals or participate in Twitter chats about work-life balance.

5. Validate Your Niche Idea
- Based on your research, assess whether there is sufficient demand and interest in your niche.
- Look for signs of a hungry market, such as high search volume, active online communities, and engaged competitors.

- Consider whether you can realistically compete and differentiate yourself in the market.
- Example: If your research reveals a thriving market for mindfulness and self-care products and services, with room for a unique angle or offering, you may have found a winner!

Now, I know this process can feel overwhelming, especially if you're new to market research. But trust me, it's worth investing the time and effort to ensure that you're choosing a niche with real profit potential.

And remember, this isn't a one-time thing – as you continue to build and grow your online business, you'll want to stay tuned into your market and audience, continuously refining your offerings and strategies based on their evolving needs and desires.

But for now, focus on gathering as much data and insight as possible to inform your niche selection. And don't be afraid to pivot or adjust your ideas based on what you learn – the beauty of online business is that you have the flexibility to adapt and evolve as you go.

So, roll up your sleeves, put on your research hat, and let's dig into the exciting world of market demand and competition. With a little elbow grease and a lot of curiosity, you'll be well on your way to choosing a profitable niche that sets you up for online business success!

Narrowing Down Your Niche and Validating Your Idea

Congratulations, you've done the hard work of identifying your skills, interests, and expertise, and researching market demand and competition. Now it's time to take all that juicy data and insight and use it to narrow down your niche and validate your idea. This is where the rubber meets the road, and you start to crystallize your vision for your online business.

Let's break it down:

1. Analyze Your Research
- Review all the data and insights you gathered during your market research.
- Look for patterns, trends, and opportunities that align with your skills, interests, and expertise.
- Identify the most promising niche ideas based on market demand, competition, and your unique value proposition.
- Example: If your research revealed a high demand for mindfulness and self-care products, with a gap in the market for a specific type of product or target audience, that could be a strong contender for your niche.

2. Narrow Your Focus
- Take your top niche ideas and start to narrow them down even further.
- Look for ways to specialize or niche down within your chosen market.
- Consider factors like demographics, psychographics, and specific pain points or desires.

- Example: Within the mindfulness and self-care niche, you might choose to focus specifically on busy working moms, targeting their unique challenges and needs.

3. Define Your Unique Value Proposition
- What makes your offering unique and valuable compared to competitors in your niche?
- How will you differentiate yourself and stand out in the market?
- What specific benefits or outcomes will you provide to your target audience?
- Example: As a mindfulness and self-care coach for busy working moms, your unique value proposition might be helping them find balance, reduce stress, and prioritize self-care in just 15 minutes a day.

4. Validate Your Idea
- Before you go all-in on your chosen niche, it's important to validate your idea and ensure there's real demand and interest.
- Create a simple landing page or survey to gauge interest and collect email addresses from potential customers.
- Reach out to your target audience directly and ask for feedback on your idea.
- Look for early signs of traction, such as email sign-ups, pre-orders, or positive feedback from your network.
- Example: To validate your mindfulness and self-care coaching idea, you might create a simple landing page offering a free guided meditation for busy moms, and see how many people sign up.

5. Refine and Iterate
- Based on the feedback and data you gather during the validation process, refine and iterate on your niche and offering.
- Look for ways to improve your messaging, positioning, and unique value proposition.
- Be open to pivoting or adjusting your idea based on what you learn.
- Example: If your initial validation efforts fall flat, don't be discouraged – use that feedback to refine your idea and try again until you find a winning combination.

I know this process can feel like a lot of trial and error, but that's all part of the entrepreneurial journey. The key is to stay focused on your vision, stay open to feedback and learning, and keep pushing forward until you find that sweet spot where your passions, skills, and market demand align.

And remember, even after you've validated your idea and launched your online business, the process of refining and iterating never stops. As your market and audience evolve, so too will your offerings and strategies. The most successful online entrepreneurs are the ones who stay agile, adaptable, and always learning.

So, take a deep breath, trust the process, and keep putting one foot in front of the other. With persistence, patience, and a willingness to experiment and learn, you'll be well on your way to building a thriving online business in a profitable niche that lights you up and serves your audience well.

You've got this!

Chapter 2
Understanding Different Online Business Models

E-commerce: Building an Online Store

Hey there, aspiring online entrepreneur! Now that you've got a handle on choosing your niche, it's time to dive into the exciting world of online business models. And what better place to start than with the ever-popular e-commerce model?

E-commerce, short for electronic commerce, refers to the buying and selling of goods or services over the internet. In other words, it's all about building an online store where you can showcase your products, process orders, and make money while you sleep (or, you know, while you're busy living your best life).

Let's break down the key components of building a successful e-commerce store:

1. Choose Your Products
- What will you sell in your online store? This is where your niche research comes in handy!
- Consider factors like market demand, competition, pricing, and shipping logistics.
- Decide whether you'll create your own products, source from wholesalers, or dropship from manufacturers.
- Example: If your niche is eco-friendly home goods, you might create your own line of sustainable cleaning products or partner with a wholesaler to curate a selection of green home decor items.

2. Select Your E-Commerce Platform
- There are many e-commerce platforms to choose from, each with its own features, pricing, and learning curve.
- Popular options include Shopify, WooCommerce, Magento, and BigCommerce.
- Consider factors like ease of use, customization options, payment processing, and customer support.
- Example: Shopify is a popular choice for beginners, with a user-friendly interface, built-in payment processing, and a wide range of customizable templates.

3. Design Your Online Store
- Your online store's design should reflect your brand, niche, and target audience.
- Choose a visually appealing theme or template that's easy to navigate and showcases your products effectively.
- Optimize your product descriptions, images, and categories for search engines and user experience.
- Example: For an eco-friendly home goods store, you might choose a clean, minimalist design with earth tones, high-quality product images, and clear, concise descriptions that highlight each item's sustainable features.

4. Set Up Payment Processing
- To accept payments from customers, you'll need to set up payment processing on your e-commerce platform.
- Options include PayPal, Stripe, Square, and other third-party payment gateways.
- Consider factors like transaction fees, security, and ease of use for customers.

- Example: Shopify has built-in payment processing with Shopify Payments, which offers competitive rates and a seamless checkout experience for customers.

5. Launch and Market Your Store
- Once your online store is set up and stocked with products, it's time to launch and start driving traffic!
- Use a combination of organic and paid marketing strategies to reach your target audience, such as social media, email marketing, content marketing, and paid advertising.
- Continuously test and optimize your marketing efforts to improve conversions and drive sales.
- Example: To market your eco-friendly home goods store, you might create a blog with sustainable living tips, partner with eco-conscious influencers on Instagram, and run targeted Facebook ads to green-minded consumers.

Building a successful e-commerce store takes time, effort, and a willingness to learn and adapt. But with the right niche, products, platform, and marketing strategy, the rewards can be tremendous.

Imagine waking up to sales notifications, happy customer reviews, and a growing base of loyal fans who can't get enough of your products. That's the power of e-commerce, my friend!

Of course, e-commerce is just one of many online business models you can choose from. In the coming sections, we'll explore other popular options like affiliate marketing, freelancing, digital products, and coaching/consulting. Each model has its own unique benefits, challenges, and strategies for success.

But for now, let's celebrate the exciting possibilities of e-commerce and all the ways it can help you turn your passions into profits. Whether you're a crafty creator, a savvy curator, or a branding mastermind, there's an online store out there with your name on it.

So, roll up your sleeves, get ready to hustle, and let's build an e-commerce empire together!

Affiliate Marketing: Promoting Other People's Products

Welcome back, intrepid online entrepreneur! Now that we've explored the exciting world of e-commerce, let's dive into another popular online business model: affiliate marketing. This is where you can turn your passion for promoting into profit, all while leveraging other people's products and services.

Affiliate marketing is a performance-based model where you earn commissions by promoting other companies' products or services. Essentially, you become a virtual salesperson, using your online presence and marketing skills to drive sales and earn a piece of the pie.

Here's how it works:

1. Choose Your Niche and Products
- Just like with e-commerce, your success in affiliate marketing starts with choosing the right niche and products to promote.
- Look for products or services that align with your interests, expertise, and target audience.
- Consider factors like commission rates, product quality, and market demand.
- Example: If your niche is personal finance, you might become an affiliate for budgeting apps, investment courses, or credit card offers.

2. Join Affiliate Programs
- Once you've identified potential products or services to promote, you'll need to join their affiliate programs.
- Many companies have their own in-house affiliate programs, while others use third-party networks like Amazon Associates, Commission Junction, or ShareASale.
- Follow the application process for each program, which may include providing your website or social media details, agreeing to terms and conditions, and setting up payment information.
- Example: To become an Amazon Associate, you'll need to create an account, provide your website or YouTube channel URL, and agree to their operating agreement.

3. Promote Your Affiliate Products
- Now comes the fun part: promoting your affiliate products and driving sales!
- There are many ways to promote affiliate products, such as writing product reviews, creating comparison guides, sharing affiliate links on social media, or creating video demonstrations.
- The key is to provide genuine value to your audience while naturally incorporating your affiliate links and calls-to-action.
- Example: As a personal finance affiliate, you might write a blog post comparing the top budgeting apps, including your affiliate links for readers to sign up and try them out.

4. Track Your Performance
- To optimize your affiliate marketing efforts and maximize your earnings, it's crucial to track your performance.
- Most affiliate programs provide tracking dashboards where you can see your clicks, sales, and commissions.
- Use this data to identify your top-performing products, traffic sources, and promotional strategies.
- Example: If you notice that your YouTube product reviews are driving the most sales, you might double down on that format and create more videos showcasing your affiliate products.

5. Build Trust and Authority
- The most successful affiliate marketers are those who build trust and authority with their audience.
- This means being transparent about your affiliate relationships, only promoting products you genuinely believe in, and providing honest, unbiased reviews and recommendations.
- Over time, as you establish yourself as a trusted resource in your niche, your affiliate income can grow exponentially.
- Example: In your blog's disclaimer or about page, clearly state that you use affiliate links and may earn commissions on purchases made through your recommendations.

Affiliate marketing can be a lucrative and rewarding online business model, especially if you have a knack for promotion and a passion for helping others make informed purchasing decisions.

Plus, with no inventory to manage or products to create, the startup costs and risks are relatively low.

Of course, like any business model, affiliate marketing has its challenges and competition. It takes time, effort, and strategic thinking to stand out in a crowded market and earn the trust of your audience. But with persistence, creativity, and a focus on providing genuine value, the sky's the limit!

So, if you're ready to turn your influence into income and join the exciting world of affiliate marketing, let's get started! Your dream lifestyle of passive income, flexibility, and freedom awaits.

Freelancing: Offering Your Services Online

Hey there, skilled and savvy entrepreneur! Are you ready to turn your talents into a thriving online business? Then freelancing might just be the perfect model for you! Freelancing is all about offering your services to clients online, whether that's writing, design, programming, marketing, or any other skill you've got up your sleeve.

As a freelancer, you're in charge of your own schedule, rates, and projects. You get to be your own boss, work from anywhere with an internet connection, and build a portfolio of work that showcases your expertise. Sounds pretty great, right?

Let's break down the key steps to launching and growing your freelance business online:

1. Identify Your Skills and Services
- What are you great at? What do you love doing? These are the foundation of your freelance services.
- Consider your education, work experience, and personal projects to identify your marketable skills.
- Brainstorm specific services you can offer, such as content writing, graphic design, web development, social media management, or virtual assistance.
- Example: If you're a talented writer with a background in marketing, you might offer copywriting services for businesses, including website copy, blog posts, and email newsletters.

2. Define Your Target Market
- Who are your ideal clients? What industries do they work in? What challenges do they face?
- Identifying your target market helps you tailor your services, marketing, and pricing to their specific needs.
- Consider factors like company size, budget, location, and business goals.
- Example: As a copywriter, your target market might be small to medium-sized businesses in the health and wellness industry who need help creating engaging, SEO-friendly content.

3. Create Your Online Presence
- To attract clients and showcase your work, you'll need a professional online presence.
- This typically includes a website or portfolio, social media profiles, and online directories or marketplaces.
- Your website should clearly communicate your services, skills, and experience, along with testimonials and work samples.
- Example: Create a simple website using a platform like WordPress or Squarespace, featuring your bio, services, portfolio, and contact information.

4. Set Your Rates and Pricing
- One of the trickiest parts of freelancing is determining how much to charge for your services.
- Research industry standards and competitor rates to get a baseline, but also consider your own experience, skills, and value.
- Decide whether you'll charge by the hour, by the project, or on a retainer basis.

- Example: As a new copywriter, you might charge $50-$75 per hour or $250-$500 per blog post, depending on the scope and complexity of the project.

5. Market Your Services
- To land clients and grow your business, you'll need to actively market your services.
- This can include networking on social media, reaching out to potential clients directly, guest posting or contributing to industry publications, and leveraging referrals from satisfied clients.
- Focus on showcasing your unique value proposition and the benefits you provide to your target market.
- Example: Join Facebook groups or LinkedIn communities related to your niche, offer helpful advice and insights, and share your website or portfolio when appropriate.

6. Deliver Exceptional Work
- The key to long-term success as a freelancer is consistently delivering high-quality work that meets or exceeds client expectations.
- Communicate clearly, meet deadlines, and go above and beyond to ensure client satisfaction.
- Ask for feedback and testimonials to continuously improve your services and build social proof.
- Example: For each copywriting project, start with a detailed brief or questionnaire to understand the client's goals, audience, and tone. Provide multiple revisions and edits until the client is thrilled with the final product.

Freelancing can be a fulfilling and lucrative way to build an online business around your skills and passions. With the right mindset, strategy, and hustle, you can create a sustainable income stream and a portfolio of work you're proud of.

Of course, freelancing also comes with its own set of challenges, such as managing client relationships, handling taxes and finances, and dealing with the ebbs and flows of project-based work. But with persistence, organization, and a commitment to continuous learning and growth, you can build a successful freelance business that supports your dream lifestyle.

So, if you're ready to take the leap and become your own boss, let's dive in! The world of online freelancing is waiting for you.

Digital Products: Creating and Selling Your Own Products

Well hello there, you creative genius, you! Are you ready to turn your knowledge, skills, and passion into a profitable online business? Then digital products might just be your ticket to success! Digital products are any products that can be created, delivered, and consumed online, such as ebooks, courses, templates, software, or audio/video content.

The beauty of digital products is that you create them once and can sell them over and over again, without the need for physical inventory, shipping, or production costs. Plus, you have complete control over the content, pricing, and marketing of your products, allowing you to build a business that truly reflects your unique voice and value.

Let's explore the step-by-step process of creating and selling your own digital products online:

1. Identify Your Niche and Expertise
- What topics, skills, or experiences do you have that others would find valuable?
- Consider your passions, hobbies, work experience, and areas of study.
- Look for problems or challenges your target audience faces that you can help solve with your digital products.
- Example: If you're a skilled photographer, you might create a series of Lightroom presets or a course on mastering manual mode for beginners.

2. Validate Your Product Idea
- Before investing time and energy into creating your digital product, it's essential to validate that there's a market for it.
- Research your target audience, competitors, and industry trends to ensure there's demand for your product.
- Conduct surveys, interviews, or focus groups to gather feedback and insights from potential customers.
- Example: Create a simple landing page or social media post describing your proposed photography course, and gauge interest through email sign-ups or comments.

3. Create Your Digital Product
- Once you've validated your product idea, it's time to bring it to life!
- Choose the format and delivery method that best suits your content and audience, such as a PDF ebook, video course, or software download.
- Break your content into manageable sections or modules, and create an outline or script to guide your production process.
- Invest in quality design, branding, and user experience to make your product stand out and delight your customers.
- Example: Record and edit your photography course videos using professional equipment, create accompanying worksheets and cheat sheets, and package it all in a user-friendly online course platform.

4. Price and Launch Your Product
- Determine the pricing strategy for your digital product based on its value, competition, and target audience.

- Consider factors like production costs, desired profit margin, and perceived value to the customer.
- Choose a launch strategy that builds buzz, urgency, and social proof, such as a limited-time offer, affiliate partnerships, or influencer marketing.
- Example: Price your photography course at $297, with a special launch price of $197 for the first 100 customers, and partner with photography bloggers and influencers to spread the word.

5. Market and Sell Your Product
- Now it's time to get your digital product in front of your ideal customers and start making sales!
- Leverage your existing online presence, such as your website, blog, email list, and social media channels, to promote your product.
- Experiment with paid advertising, content marketing, and partnerships to reach new audiences and drive traffic to your sales page.
- Continuously test and optimize your marketing and sales strategies based on data and customer feedback.
- Example: Create a series of blog posts and YouTube videos showcasing your photography skills and teaching beginner techniques, with calls-to-action promoting your course. Run targeted Facebook ads to photographers interested in improving their craft.

6. Deliver and Support Your Product
- Once you've made a sale, your work is just beginning! It's crucial to deliver a high-quality product and customer experience.

- Ensure your product is easily accessible, downloadable, and compatible with your customers' devices and preferences.
- Provide clear instructions, support, and resources to help your customers get the most value from your product.
- Gather feedback, testimonials, and reviews to continuously improve your product and build social proof for future sales.
- Example: Host your photography course on a user-friendly platform like Teachable or Thinkific, with clear onboarding instructions and responsive customer support. Encourage students to share their course projects and successes in a private Facebook group or community.

Creating and selling digital products can be a rewarding and scalable way to build an online business around your unique knowledge and skills. With low overhead costs, automated delivery, and endless possibilities for creativity and impact, digital products offer a powerful pathway to entrepreneurial freedom.

Of course, success with digital products requires hard work, strategic planning, and a willingness to experiment and adapt. But with persistence, passion, and a commitment to providing genuine value to your customers, you can build a thriving digital product business that supports your dreams and makes a difference in the world.

So, what are you waiting for, you digital dynamo? Let's get creating and start turning your ideas into income!

Coaching and Consulting: Sharing Your Expertise

Well, well, well, if it isn't the expert extraordinaire! Are you ready to take your knowledge, skills, and experience to the next level and make a real impact in people's lives? Then coaching and consulting might just be your calling! Coaching and consulting are all about sharing your expertise with others, helping them achieve their goals, overcome challenges, and unlock their full potential.

As a coach or consultant, you become a trusted advisor, mentor, and guide to your clients, using your unique insights and strategies to help them succeed in their personal or professional lives. Whether you specialize in business, health, relationships, or any other area of life, coaching and consulting offer a powerful way to monetize your expertise and make a difference in the world.

Let's dive into the key aspects of building a thriving coaching or consulting business online:

1. Define Your Niche and Ideal Client
- What specific area of expertise do you want to focus on in your coaching or consulting practice?
- Who are your ideal clients, and what challenges or goals do they have that you can help with?
- Consider your own background, experiences, and passions to identify a niche that aligns with your strengths and values.

- Example: If you're a experienced marketing professional, you might specialize in helping small business owners create and execute effective marketing strategies to grow their revenue and reach.

2. Develop Your Coaching or Consulting Offer
- What specific services, packages, or programs will you offer to your clients?
- Will you provide one-on-one coaching sessions, group coaching, online courses, or a combination of offerings?
- Clearly define the structure, duration, and deliverables of your coaching or consulting services, and how they provide value to your clients.
- Example: Create a 90-day coaching program that includes weekly one-on-one sessions, a customized marketing plan, and access to a private online community for support and accountability.

3. Establish Your Credibility and Authority
- To attract and retain clients, it's essential to demonstrate your credibility and authority in your niche.
- Showcase your relevant education, certifications, and experience on your website and marketing materials.
- Share case studies, testimonials, and success stories from previous clients to provide social proof and build trust.
- Publish valuable content, such as blog posts, videos, or podcasts, that showcase your expertise and provide valuable insights to your target audience.
- Example: Create a series of YouTube videos sharing marketing tips and strategies for small businesses, and feature testimonials from satisfied clients on your website.

4. Price and Package Your Services
- Determine the pricing and packaging strategy for your coaching or consulting services based on your target market, value proposition, and financial goals.
- Consider factors like your experience level, the complexity and duration of your offerings, and the results you help your clients achieve.
- Offer a range of pricing options and payment plans to accommodate different budgets and preferences, such as hourly rates, package deals, or recurring subscriptions.
- Example: Price your 90-day coaching program at $2,500, with the option for clients to pay in full or in three monthly installments of $900.

5. Market and Sell Your Services
- To attract and enroll clients, you'll need to actively market and sell your coaching or consulting services.
- Leverage your online presence, such as your website, social media profiles, and email list, to promote your offerings and engage with potential clients.
- Attend networking events, speak at conferences, or guest post on relevant blogs to expand your reach and build relationships with your target audience.
- Offer free consultations, webinars, or resources to demonstrate your value and encourage prospects to invest in your paid services.
- Example: Host a free webinar on "The 5 Essential Elements of a Successful Small Business Marketing Strategy," and invite attendees to schedule a complimentary consultation to discuss their specific needs and goals.

6. Deliver and Optimize Your Services
- Once you've enrolled a client, it's time to deliver an exceptional coaching or consulting experience that helps them achieve their desired results.
- Use a structured, yet flexible approach to your coaching or consulting sessions, with clear agendas, action items, and milestones.
- Provide ongoing support, accountability, and resources to help your clients stay motivated and on track towards their goals.
- Continuously gather feedback and data to optimize your services, improve your results, and enhance your client experience.
- Example: Use a project management tool like Asana or Trello to keep track of your client's progress and deliverables, and send regular check-in emails to provide encouragement and support.

Coaching and consulting can be a fulfilling and lucrative way to share your expertise and make a positive impact in people's lives. With the right niche, offer, and marketing strategy, you can build a thriving online business that allows you to work with clients you love, on your own terms.

Of course, success as a coach or consultant requires more than just expertise – it also takes empathy, communication skills, and a genuine commitment to your clients' success. But with dedication, integrity, and a willingness to continuously learn and grow, you can build a reputation as a trusted advisor and change-maker in your field.

Identifying Your Skills, Interests, and Expertise

Hey there, my multi-talented friend! Before we dive into the exciting world of online business, let's take a moment to focus on the most important asset you have: YOU! Identifying your unique skills, interests, and expertise is the foundation of building a successful and fulfilling online business. After all, when you align your business with your passions and strengths, work becomes play, and success becomes inevitable.

So, let's embark on a journey of self-discovery and uncover the superpowers that will fuel your entrepreneurial journey!

1. Reflect on Your Past Experiences
- Think back on your personal and professional experiences, and identify the moments when you felt most alive, engaged, and proud of your accomplishments.
- What activities, projects, or roles did you excel in and enjoy the most?
- Consider your education, hobbies, volunteer work, and any other experiences that have shaped your skills and interests.
- Example: If you've always loved writing and received praise for your college essays or work presentations, that's a strong indication of your writing skills and potential to create content-based businesses.

2. Assess Your Natural Talents and Strengths
- What comes naturally to you? What do you find easy or intuitive that others might struggle with?

- Ask friends, family, or colleagues for their honest feedback on your strengths and the unique value you bring to the table.
- Take personality assessments or strengths finder tests to gain insights into your natural abilities and working style.
- Example: If you've always been the go-to person for tech support among your friends and family, you might have a natural talent for problem-solving and teaching others about technology.

3. Identify Your Passions and Interests
- What topics or activities light you up and make you lose track of time?
- What do you love learning about, discussing, or creating in your free time?
- Consider the books, podcasts, or websites you consume regularly, and the hobbies or causes you're passionate about.
- Example: If you spend hours researching and experimenting with healthy recipes and nutrition tips, you might have a passion for wellness and a potential niche in the health coaching space.

4. Combine Your Skills, Interests, and Expertise
- Look for the intersection between your skills, interests, and experiences to identify your unique zone of genius.
- Consider how you can combine your diverse talents and passions to create a unique value proposition and stand out in the online business world.

- Brainstorm potential business ideas or niches that align with your skills, interests, and expertise, and that you would be excited to pursue long-term.
- Example: If you have a background in finance, a passion for personal development, and a talent for public speaking, you could create a business as a financial coach, helping people transform their money mindset and achieve their goals.

5. Validate Your Skills and Expertise
- Once you've identified your potential skills and expertise, it's important to validate them through real-world experience and feedback.
- Look for opportunities to practice and demonstrate your skills, whether through freelance projects, volunteer work, or personal experiments.
- Seek out mentors, peers, or clients who can provide honest feedback and help you refine your skills and expertise over time.
- Example: If you're interested in becoming a social media consultant, offer to manage the social media accounts of a local small business or non-profit for free, and track your results and learnings.

Remember, identifying your skills, interests, and expertise is an ongoing process of self-discovery and growth. As you gain more experience and knowledge, you may uncover new passions or develop new skills that shape your online business journey.

The key is to stay curious, open-minded, and willing to experiment with different ideas and approaches. Trust that by aligning your business with your unique gifts and passions, you'll not only achieve success, but also fulfillment and joy in your work.

So, take some time to reflect, explore, and celebrate all the amazing skills, interests, and experiences that make you uniquely you. Your online business adventure awaits, and it all starts with embracing your inner genius!

Chapter 3
Setting Up Your Online Business Foundation

Choosing a Domain Name and Web Hosting

Alright, my aspiring online entrepreneur! Now that you've identified your niche and business model, it's time to lay the groundwork for your online empire. And that all starts with choosing the perfect domain name and web hosting provider. Your domain name and web hosting are like the virtual real estate of your online business – they're where you'll build your website, store your content, and welcome your eager customers.

So, let's break down the process of choosing a domain name and web hosting that will set your business up for success!

1. Brainstorm Your Domain Name
- Your domain name is the web address that people will use to find your website, so it's important to choose one that's memorable, relevant, and easy to spell.
- Brainstorm a list of potential domain names that relate to your business name, niche, or unique value proposition.
- Keep it short, sweet, and simple – aim for 1-3 words that are easy to pronounce and spell, and avoid hyphens, numbers, or special characters if possible.

- Example: If your business is a wellness coaching service called "Healthy Haven," you might brainstorm domain names like healthyhaven.com, wellnesshaven.com, or healthyhavenwellness.com.

2. Check Domain Availability
- Once you have a list of potential domain names, it's time to check their availability using a domain registrar like GoDaddy, Namecheap, or Google Domains.
- Simply enter your desired domain name into the registrar's search bar, and it will let you know if it's available for purchase or if it's already taken.
- If your first choice is taken, don't worry – you can try variations or alternative extensions (like .net, .co, or .wellness) until you find an available domain that fits your brand.
- Example: If healthyhaven.com is taken, you might try healthyhaven.net, healthyhavencoaching.com, or healthyhaven.wellness.

3. Register Your Domain Name
- Once you've found an available domain name that you love, it's time to make it officially yours by registering it with a domain registrar.
- Most domain registrars offer easy step-by-step instructions for registering your domain, which typically involves providing your contact information and paying an annual registration fee (usually around $10-15 per year).

- Be sure to choose a reputable registrar with good customer support and security features, and consider adding privacy protection to keep your personal information hidden from public records.
- Example: To register healthyhaven.com, you would create an account with a registrar like GoDaddy, search for the domain name, add it to your cart, and complete the checkout process with your payment and contact details.

4. Choose Your Web Hosting Provider
- Now that you have your domain name, it's time to choose a web hosting provider that will store your website files and make them accessible to visitors on the internet.
- There are many types of web hosting available, from shared hosting (where your site shares server space with other sites) to dedicated hosting (where you have your own private server). The right choice for you will depend on your website's needs, traffic, and budget.
- Look for a hosting provider with good uptime, fast loading speeds, easy-to-use control panels, and responsive customer support. Some popular options include Bluehost, SiteGround, and HostGator.
- Example: If you're just starting out with a small coaching website, you might choose a shared hosting plan from Bluehost that includes free domain registration, one-click WordPress installation, and 24/7 customer support for around $5-10 per month.

5. Connect Your Domain and Hosting
- Once you've registered your domain and chosen your web hosting provider, the final step is to connect the two so that your domain points to your website files on your hosting account.
- Most hosting providers offer easy instructions for connecting your domain, which typically involves updating your domain's DNS (Domain Name System) settings to point to your hosting provider's nameservers.
- This process can take up to 48 hours to fully propagate, but once it's done, your domain will be live and ready for you to start building your website!
- Example: In your Bluehost control panel, you would enter your registered domain name (healthyhaven.com) and update the DNS settings to point to Bluehost's nameservers. Then, you can install WordPress and start designing your website!

Choosing your domain name and web hosting provider is an exciting step in building your online business foundation. It's like laying the first brick in your virtual storefront, and watching your business come to life online.

Of course, there are many other technical details and decisions involved in setting up your website, from choosing a website platform to designing your layout and branding. But by starting with a strong domain name and reliable hosting provider, you'll be well on your way to creating an online presence that attracts and delights your ideal customers.

So, take your time, do your research, and choose a domain name and hosting provider that aligns with your business goals and values. And remember, your website is a constant work in progress – you can always make changes and improvements as your business grows and evolves over time.

Now, let's get ready to build something amazing!

Designing Your Website and Branding

Congratulations, my brilliant entrepreneur! You've secured your domain name and web hosting, and now it's time for the fun part: designing your website and creating a brand that will make your business shine online. Your website and branding are like the virtual storefront and packaging of your business – they're what will attract, engage, and delight your ideal customers from the moment they land on your site.

So, let's dive into the key elements of designing a website and brand that truly represents your unique business and personality!

1. Define Your Brand Identity
- Before you start designing your website, it's important to have a clear understanding of your brand identity – the visual and emotional essence of your business.
- Consider your business name, logo, color palette, typography, imagery, and tone of voice – how do you want your brand to look, feel, and sound to your target audience?
- Create a brand style guide that outlines these elements and ensures consistency across all your online and offline marketing materials.
- Example: For your wellness coaching business, "Healthy Haven," you might choose a soothing color palette of greens and blues, a nature-inspired logo with a leaf or tree symbol, and a warm, supportive tone of voice.

2. Choose Your Website Platform
- With your brand identity in mind, it's time to choose a website platform that will allow you to easily design and customize your site to match your vision.
- There are many website builders and content management systems (CMS) available, from user-friendly options like Wix, Squarespace, and WordPress.com to more flexible, self-hosted platforms like WordPress.org.
- Consider factors like ease of use, design flexibility, e-commerce capabilities, and scalability when choosing your platform.
- Example: For a small coaching business, you might start with a simple, drag-and-drop website builder like Squarespace, which offers beautiful templates and easy customization options.

3. Select a Website Template or Theme
- Once you've chosen your website platform, it's time to select a template or theme that will serve as the foundation for your site's design.
- Look for a template that aligns with your brand identity and business goals, with a layout and features that will showcase your content and services effectively.
- Consider factors like responsiveness (how well the site looks on mobile devices), customization options, and built-in features like contact forms, social media integration, and blog functionality.
- Example: Within Squarespace, you might choose the "Motto" template, which offers a clean, minimalist design with plenty of white space, beautiful typography, and a simple navigation menu.

4. Customize Your Website Design

- With your template selected, it's time to customize your website design to truly make it your own.
- Use your brand style guide to inform your color choices, typography, imagery, and overall aesthetic – your site should feel cohesive and consistent with your brand identity.
- Pay attention to key pages like your homepage, about page, services page, and contact page – these are often the first places visitors will land and form impressions of your business.
- Example: On your Healthy Haven homepage, you might feature a large, inviting hero image of a serene nature scene, with a clear headline that communicates your unique value proposition and a prominent call-to-action button to book a free consultation.

5. Create Compelling Website Content

- With your website design in place, it's time to fill your site with compelling, engaging content that will inform, inspire, and convert your visitors into customers.
- Write clear, concise, and persuasive copy that communicates your brand voice and value proposition, and guides visitors through your site towards your desired actions (like booking a service or joining your email list).
- Use high-quality, relevant images and videos to break up your text, illustrate your points, and create an emotional connection with your audience.

- Optimize your content for search engines by including relevant keywords, meta descriptions, and alt tags – this will help your site rank higher in search results and attract more organic traffic.
- Example: On your Healthy Haven blog, you might write a series of informative, keyword-rich articles on topics like "10 Simple Ways to Reduce Stress and Find Inner Peace" or "The Benefits of Mindfulness Meditation for Busy Professionals."

Designing your website and branding is a creative, iterative process that allows you to express your unique business identity and connect with your ideal customers online. It's an opportunity to create a virtual space that feels authentic, inviting, and valuable to your target audience – a space where they can learn, grow, and transform through your offerings.

Of course, designing a website and brand is just the beginning – the real magic happens when you start attracting, engaging, and serving your customers through your site. But by laying a strong foundation with a clear brand identity, user-friendly website platform, and compelling content, you'll be well on your way to building a thriving online business that makes a positive impact in the world.

So, let your creativity flow, stay true to your vision and values, and have fun bringing your brand to life online. Your ideal customers are out there, waiting to discover the unique gifts and services that only you can offer – and your website is the key to connecting with them and building lasting relationships.

Now, let's get designing and create something beautiful together!

Essential Tools and Software for Running Your Business

Alright, my savvy entrepreneur! Now that you've designed a stunning website and brand for your online business, it's time to talk about the behind-the-scenes tools and software that will keep your operations running smoothly and efficiently. Just like a chef needs a well-equipped kitchen or a musician needs a tuned instrument, you need a toolkit of reliable, powerful software to manage, automate, and grow your business online.

So, let's explore some of the essential tools and software that every online business owner should have in their arsenal!

1. Email Marketing Software
- Email marketing is one of the most effective ways to build relationships, nurture leads, and drive sales for your online business.
- You'll need an email marketing software that allows you to easily create, send, and track email campaigns, newsletters, and automated sequences to your subscribers.
- Popular options include Mailchimp, ConvertKit, and ActiveCampaign – each with their own unique features and pricing plans.
- Example: With Mailchimp, you can create beautiful, branded email templates, segment your subscribers based on their interests and behaviors, and track your open rates, click-through rates, and other key metrics.

2. Social Media Management Tools
- Social media is a powerful tool for building brand awareness, engaging with your audience, and driving traffic to your website.
- But managing multiple social media accounts can be time-consuming and overwhelming – that's where social media management tools come in.
- Tools like Hootsuite, Sprout Social, and Buffer allow you to schedule posts in advance, monitor your social media mentions and messages, and analyze your performance across all your accounts in one dashboard.
- Example: With Hootsuite, you can create a content calendar for all your social media accounts, schedule posts for optimal times, and track your likes, comments, and shares across platforms.

3. Project Management Software
- As your online business grows, you'll likely be juggling multiple projects, tasks, and deadlines at once – and that's where project management software can be a lifesaver.
- Tools like Asana, Trello, and Basecamp allow you to create projects, assign tasks to team members, set due dates, and track progress all in one centralized platform.
- This can help you stay organized, prioritize your workload, and collaborate more efficiently with your team or clients.
- Example: With Asana, you can create a project for your next online course launch, break it down into subtasks and milestones, assign responsibilities to your team members, and track your progress with visual dashboards and reports.

4. Customer Relationship Management (CRM) Software

- As you attract more leads and customers to your online business, it's important to have a system in place for managing and nurturing those relationships over time.
- That's where customer relationship management (CRM) software comes in – tools like Salesforce, HubSpot, and Zoho allow you to store and organize your customer data, track your interactions and communications, and automate your sales and marketing processes.
- This can help you provide better customer service, identify upsell and cross-sell opportunities, and ultimately drive more revenue for your business.
- Example: With HubSpot, you can create a centralized database of your leads and customers, track their website behavior and email engagement, and use that data to send targeted, personalized marketing campaigns and sales outreach.

5. Analytics and Tracking Tools

- To make data-driven decisions and continually optimize your online business, you need reliable analytics and tracking tools that give you insights into your website traffic, user behavior, and marketing performance.
- Tools like Google Analytics, Hotjar, and Mixpanel allow you to track your website visitors, page views, bounce rates, conversion rates, and other key metrics that can help you identify areas for improvement and growth.
- You can also use these tools to set up goals and funnels, run A/B tests, and track the ROI of your marketing campaigns across different channels and platforms.

- Example: With Google Analytics, you can set up tracking codes on your website to monitor your traffic sources, user demographics, behavior flows, and conversion rates – and use that data to make informed decisions about your content, design, and marketing strategies.

Investing in the right tools and software for your online business is like building a strong foundation for a house – it may not be the most glamorous or visible part of the process, but it's essential for the stability, functionality, and growth of your business over time.

Of course, every business is unique, and you may not need all of these tools right away – but by familiarizing yourself with the options and gradually incorporating them into your workflows, you'll be able to streamline your operations, save time and energy, and focus on what you do best: serving your customers and growing your business.

So, take some time to research and experiment with different tools and software, and don't be afraid to invest in the ones that will truly support and accelerate your business goals. With the right toolkit in place, you'll be unstoppable!

Now, let's get back to building your online empire, one tool at a time!

Legal Requirements and Business Registration

Congratulations, my enterprising friend! You've got your website, your branding, and your essential tools all set up – now it's time to dot your i's, cross your t's, and make sure your online business is legally legit. I know, I know – legal stuff can be about as exciting as watching paint dry, but trust me, it's crucial for protecting your business, your assets, and your peace of mind in the long run.

So, let's break down the key legal requirements and business registration steps you need to take to set your online business up for success!

1. Choose Your Business Structure
- One of the first legal decisions you'll need to make is choosing the right business structure for your online business.
- The most common options are sole proprietorship, partnership, limited liability company (LLC), and corporation – each with their own pros, cons, and tax implications.
- Factors to consider include your business size, ownership, liability protection, and growth plans.
- Example: If you're a solopreneur running a small coaching business, a sole proprietorship may be the simplest and most cost-effective option. But if you're planning to scale your business and hire employees, an LLC or corporation may offer more liability protection and tax benefits.

2. Register Your Business Name
- Once you've chosen your business structure, you'll need to register your business name with your state or local government.
- This typically involves searching for available names, filling out a registration form, and paying a filing fee.
- You may also need to register for a trademark or domain name to protect your brand and intellectual property.
- Example: To register your business name as an LLC in California, you would need to search the California Secretary of State's business entity database, file Articles of Organization, and pay a filing fee of $70.

3. Obtain Business Licenses and Permits
- Depending on your business type and location, you may need to obtain various business licenses and permits to operate legally.
- These may include a general business license, professional licenses (e.g. for coaching or consulting), sales tax permits, health permits, and zoning permits.
- You can usually find information on required licenses and permits on your state or local government's website, or by contacting your local Small Business Administration (SBA) office.
- Example: If you're running an online food delivery business in New York City, you may need to obtain a Food Service Establishment Permit from the NYC Department of Health and Mental Hygiene, as well as a sales tax permit from the New York State Department of Taxation and Finance.

4. Set Up Your Business Finances

- To keep your personal and business finances separate and make tax time a breeze, it's important to set up dedicated business banking and credit accounts.
- This typically involves opening a business checking account, obtaining a business credit card or line of credit, and setting up a bookkeeping system to track your income and expenses.
- You may also need to obtain an Employer Identification Number (EIN) from the IRS, which is like a social security number for your business and is required for opening bank accounts, filing taxes, and hiring employees.
- Example: You could open a business checking account with Chase Bank, which offers online banking, mobile deposits, and integration with popular accounting software like QuickBooks or FreshBooks.

5. Understand Your Tax Obligations

- As a business owner, you'll be responsible for paying various federal, state, and local taxes, depending on your business structure and location.
- These may include income taxes, self-employment taxes, sales taxes, and payroll taxes (if you have employees).
- It's important to understand your tax obligations, set aside money for estimated tax payments, and keep accurate records of your income and expenses throughout the year.

Example: If you're a sole proprietor, you'll need to report your business income and expenses on Schedule C of your personal income tax return, and pay self-employment taxes (Social Security and Medicare) on your net profit.

I know this is a lot of information to take in, and the legal side of starting an online business can feel overwhelming at times. But by taking it step by step, seeking guidance from professionals (like lawyers and accountants), and staying organized and compliant, you'll be setting your business up for long-term success and minimizing your legal risks.

Remember, the legal foundation of your business is just as important as your website, your marketing, and your products or services. It's what allows you to operate with confidence, credibility, and integrity – and that's priceless.

So, take a deep breath, grab a cup of coffee (or a glass of wine, if that's more your style), and let's tackle these legal requirements one at a time. Your future self (and your business) will thank you!

Now, let's get back to building your online empire, legally and responsibly!

Chapter 4
Mastering Search Engine Optimization (SEO)

Understanding How Search Engines Work

Welcome back, my SEO-savvy friend! Now that you've got your online business legally set up and ready to roll, it's time to dive into the exciting world of search engine optimization (SEO). SEO is like the secret sauce that can take your website from invisible to invincible – it's what helps your ideal customers find you online, fall in love with your brand, and become loyal fans and advocates.

But before we get into the nitty-gritty of keywords, backlinks, and meta tags, let's take a step back and understand how search engines actually work. Because once you know the rules of the game, you can start playing to win!

1. Crawling
- The first step in the search engine process is called "crawling" – this is when search engine bots (also known as "spiders" or "crawlers") visit and scan websites across the internet.
- These bots follow links from page to page, discovering and indexing new content along the way.
- They also check for updates and changes to existing pages, to keep their database fresh and relevant.

- Example: When you publish a new blog post on your website, Google's crawlers will eventually find and scan it, adding it to their index of web pages.

2. Indexing
- Once the crawlers have discovered and scanned a web page, they store its content and metadata in a massive database called an "index".
- This index is like a giant library catalog of all the web pages on the internet, organized by keywords, topics, and relevance.
- When a user types a search query into a search engine, the engine searches its index for the most relevant and authoritative pages to display in the search results.
- Example: If a user searches for "vegan recipes", the search engine will scan its index for web pages that contain those keywords, have high-quality content and backlinks, and are optimized for relevance and user experience.

3. Ranking
- The final step in the search engine process is ranking – this is when the search engine determines the order in which to display the relevant web pages in the search results.
- Search engines use complex algorithms to rank pages based on hundreds of factors, including:
- Relevance: How closely the page matches the user's search query and intent
- Authority: How trustworthy and credible the page and website are, based on factors like backlinks, domain age, and social shares

- User experience: How easy and enjoyable the page is to use and navigate, based on factors like mobile-friendliness, page speed, and bounce rate
- The goal of the search engine is to provide the most useful, relevant, and satisfying results to the user – so the pages that best meet those criteria will rank higher in the search results.
- Example: If your vegan recipe blog post is well-written, includes relevant keywords, has high-quality backlinks from other food blogs, loads quickly on mobile devices, and keeps users engaged on your site – it has a good chance of ranking high in the search results for related queries.

As you can see, search engines are incredibly complex and sophisticated systems – but at their core, they're all about matching users with the best possible answers to their questions. And as an online business owner, your job is to create and optimize content that meets those needs better than anyone else in your niche.

Of course, mastering SEO takes time, effort, and constant learning – search engine algorithms are always evolving, and what works today may not work tomorrow. But by understanding the basics of how search engines work, and focusing on creating high-quality, user-friendly, and keyword-optimized content, you'll be well on your way to SEO success.

So, put on your detective hat, grab your magnifying glass, and let's start exploring the fascinating world of search engine optimization together!

Keyword Research and Analysis

Alright, my keyword-curious friend! Now that you understand how search engines work, it's time to dive into the heart of SEO: keyword research and analysis. Keywords are the foundation of your SEO strategy – they're the words and phrases that your ideal customers use when searching for products, services, or information related to your business. And by identifying and targeting the right keywords, you can attract more qualified traffic, boost your search rankings, and grow your online presence like never before. ■

So, let's break down the process of keyword research and analysis, step by step!

1. Brainstorm Your Seed Keywords
- The first step in keyword research is to brainstorm a list of "seed keywords" – these are broad, high-level terms that describe your business, products, or services.
- Put yourself in your ideal customer's shoes – what words or phrases would they use to search for what you offer?
- Consider factors like your niche, location, unique selling proposition, and customer pain points.
- Example: If you run a vegan recipe blog, your seed keywords might include terms like "vegan recipes", "plant-based cooking", "healthy vegan meals", and "easy vegan desserts".

2. Use Keyword Research Tools
- Once you have your seed keywords, it's time to expand and refine your list using keyword research tools.
- These tools can help you discover related keywords, analyze search volume and competition, and identify long-tail keyword opportunities.
- Some popular keyword research tools include:
- Google Keyword Planner: A free tool that provides keyword ideas and search volume data based on your seed keywords and website.
- SEMrush: A paid tool that offers in-depth keyword research, competitor analysis, and content optimization features.
- Ahrefs: Another paid tool that provides comprehensive keyword data, backlink analysis, and content exploration features.
- Example: Using Google Keyword Planner, you might discover related keywords like "vegan meal prep", "vegan baking tips", and "vegan protein sources" – along with their average monthly search volumes and competition levels.

3. Analyze Keyword Metrics
- As you build your keyword list, it's important to analyze and prioritize your keywords based on key metrics like:
- Search Volume: The average number of times a keyword is searched per month – higher volume means more potential traffic.
- Keyword Difficulty: A score that estimates how hard it would be to rank for a keyword based on factors like competition and authority – lower difficulty means easier ranking potential.

- Click-Through Rate (CTR): The percentage of searchers who click on a search result for a given keyword – higher CTR means more engagement and relevance.
- By analyzing these metrics, you can identify the keywords that offer the best balance of volume, competition, and relevance for your business.
- Example: For your vegan recipe blog, you might prioritize keywords like "easy vegan breakfast ideas" (high volume, low difficulty, high CTR) over keywords like "vegan" (high volume, high difficulty, low CTR).

4. Map Keywords to Content
- Once you have your prioritized keyword list, it's time to map those keywords to your website content.
- Look for opportunities to optimize your existing pages for your target keywords, as well as gaps where you could create new content to target untapped keyword opportunities.
- Consider factors like search intent (what the searcher is looking for), content type (blog post, product page, etc.), and content format (text, video, infographic, etc.).
- Example: For the keyword "easy vegan breakfast ideas", you might create a new blog post titled "10 Quick and Easy Vegan Breakfast Recipes for Busy Mornings" – optimized with the target keyword in the title, headings, and throughout the content.

By conducting thorough keyword research and analysis, you can create a roadmap for your SEO strategy – one that attracts the right people, to the right pages, at the right time.

And as you implement and refine your keyword strategy over time, you'll start to see the compounding effects of higher rankings, more traffic, and more conversions.

Of course, keyword research is just one piece of the SEO puzzle – you also need to consider factors like on-page optimization, link building, and technical SEO (which we'll cover in future sections). But by starting with a solid foundation of relevant, high-opportunity keywords, you'll be setting yourself up for long-term SEO success.

So, grab your thinking cap, fire up your favorite keyword research tool, and let's start uncovering the hidden gems in your niche!

On-Page SEO: Optimizing Your Website's Content and Structure

Welcome back, my optimization-obsessed friend! Now that you've mastered the art of keyword research and analysis, it's time to put those insights into action with on-page SEO. On-page SEO refers to all the techniques and best practices you can use to optimize your website's content and structure for search engines – from crafting compelling titles and meta descriptions to structuring your content with headers and internal links. And when you get your on-page SEO right, you'll be rewarded with higher search rankings, more organic traffic, and better user engagement.

So, let's dive into the key elements of on-page SEO and how you can use them to supercharge your website's performance!

1. Title Tags and Meta Descriptions
- Your title tag and meta description are the first things that searchers see in the search results – and they can make or break your click-through rates.
- Your title tag should be a concise, compelling, and keyword-rich summary of your page's content – ideally under 60 characters.
- Your meta description should be a longer, more detailed snippet that entices searchers to click through to your page – ideally under 160 characters.
- Example: For your "easy vegan breakfast ideas" blog post, your title tag might be "10 Quick and Easy Vegan Breakfast Recipes | Your Blog Name", and your meta description might be "Looking for delicious and easy

- vegan breakfast ideas? Check out our roundup of 10 quick and healthy recipes that will fuel your day and satisfy your taste buds!"

2. Header Tags and Content Structure
- Header tags (H1, H2, H3, etc.) are used to structure your content into clear, hierarchical sections – making it easier for both search engines and users to understand and navigate.
- Your H1 tag should be your page's main title, and should include your primary keyword.
- Your H2-H6 tags should be used to break up your content into smaller, more specific sections – each with its own keyword-optimized subheading.
- Example: For your "easy vegan breakfast ideas" blog post, your H1 tag might be "10 Quick and Easy Vegan Breakfast Recipes", and your H2 tags might include "1. Overnight Oats with Chia Seeds and Berries", "2. Tofu Scramble with Veggies", etc.

3. Keyword Optimization
- To rank for your target keywords, you need to optimize your content with those keywords in strategic locations – without going overboard and risking keyword stuffing.
- Include your primary keyword in your title tag, meta description, H1 tag, and first paragraph of your content.
- Use variations and long-tail versions of your keyword throughout your content, in a natural and contextual way.

Example: For your "easy vegan breakfast ideas" blog post, you might use variations like "quick vegan breakfast recipes", "healthy plant-based breakfast ideas", and "vegan breakfast on the go" throughout your content.

4. Content Quality and Length
- While keyword optimization is important, the quality and length of your content are even more critical for on-page SEO.
- Search engines prioritize content that is in-depth, well-researched, and provides unique value to users.
- Aim for a minimum of 1000-1500 words per page, and use a mix of text, images, videos, and other media to keep users engaged.
- Example: For your "easy vegan breakfast ideas" blog post, you might include detailed recipe instructions, nutritional information, and step-by-step photos or videos to make your content as helpful and engaging as possible.

5. Internal Linking and Site Structure
- Internal linking is the practice of linking from one page on your site to another – and it's crucial for both SEO and user experience.
- By linking to relevant, high-authority pages on your site, you can boost those pages' search rankings and help users discover more of your content.
- Your site structure should be logical, hierarchical, and easy to navigate – with clear categories and subcategories for your content.

- Example: For your "easy vegan breakfast ideas" blog post, you might link to other relevant recipes on your site, as well as your main "Recipes" category page and your "About" page.

By implementing these on-page SEO techniques consistently across your website, you'll be sending all the right signals to search engines – and more importantly, providing a better, more valuable experience for your users. And when you combine on-page optimization with other key SEO strategies like link building and technical optimization (which we'll cover next), you'll be unstoppable!

Of course, on-page SEO is an ongoing process – as you create new content and update existing pages, you'll need to continually refine your optimization strategy based on your target keywords, user feedback, and search engine guidelines. But by making on-page SEO a core part of your content creation process, you'll be setting yourself up for long-term, sustainable search success.

So, roll up your sleeves, put on your optimization hat, and let's start crafting some irresistibly clickable, search-friendly content together!

Off-Page SEO: Building Quality Backlinks and Improving Your Site's Authority

Hey there, my link-building legend! Are you ready to take your SEO game to the next level? Because today, we're diving into the exciting world of off-page SEO – the strategies and tactics you can use to build your website's authority, credibility, and search rankings from the outside in. Off-page SEO is all about building high-quality backlinks from other reputable websites to your own – essentially, getting other people to vouch for your awesomeness online. And when you do it right, you'll be rewarded with higher domain authority, more referral traffic, and better overall search performance.

So, let's explore some of the most effective off-page SEO techniques and how you can use them to skyrocket your site's authority and visibility!

1. Guest Posting
- Guest posting is the practice of writing content for other websites in your niche – and including a backlink to your own site within that content.
- By guest posting on high-quality, relevant sites, you can tap into new audiences, build relationships with other influencers, and earn valuable backlinks to your site.
- Look for guest posting opportunities on sites that have high domain authority, engaged audiences, and content that complements your own expertise and niche.

- Example: As a vegan recipe blogger, you might guest post on popular health and wellness sites like Mind Body Green or The Kitchn – sharing your delicious recipes and linking back to your own blog for more plant-based inspiration.

2. Broken Link Building
- Broken link building is a technique where you find broken links (links that no longer work) on other websites – and then reach out to the site owner to suggest replacing those links with links to your own relevant content.
- This strategy works because site owners are often grateful for the heads up about broken links on their site – and more than happy to replace them with high-quality, relevant alternatives.
- Use tools like Ahrefs or Check My Links to find broken links on sites in your niche – and then create content that would be a good fit to replace those links.
- Example: If you find a broken link to a recipe for "vegan chocolate chip cookies" on a popular food blog, you might reach out to the blog owner and suggest replacing that link with a link to your own amazing vegan chocolate chip cookie recipe.

3. Skyscraper Content
- The skyscraper technique is a content-based link building strategy where you find popular, high-performing content in your niche – and then create an even better, more comprehensive version of that content on your own site.

- By creating the definitive, go-to resource on a particular topic, you can attract backlinks from other sites that want to reference and share your incredible content.
- Use tools like BuzzSumo or Ahrefs Content Explorer to find the most shared and linked-to content in your niche – and then brainstorm ways to create an even more epic, in-depth version of that content.
- Example: If the top-performing post for "vegan meal prep ideas" is a list of 10 recipes, you might create a mega-post with 50 recipes, complete with grocery lists, nutritional info, and meal prep tips and tricks.

4. Influencer Outreach

- Influencer outreach is the process of building relationships with key influencers, bloggers, and thought leaders in your niche – and getting them to share and link to your content.
- By getting endorsements and backlinks from respected influencers, you can boost your own site's credibility and authority – and tap into their engaged followings.
- Identify influencers who align with your brand values and content themes – and then reach out to them with personalized, value-driven pitches for collaboration or content sharing.
- Example: As a vegan recipe blogger, you might reach out to popular vegan YouTubers or Instagram influencers – offering to create custom recipes or content features for their channels, in exchange for a backlink and shoutout to your blog.

5. Community Building
- Finally, one of the most powerful off-page SEO strategies is simply building a strong, engaged community around your brand and content.
- By creating valuable resources, fostering meaningful discussions, and providing exceptional customer service, you can turn your website into a go-to destination for your niche – and attract natural, high-quality backlinks as a result.
- Participate in online forums, social media groups, and Q&A sites related to your niche – providing helpful answers and resources (and occasionally linking back to your own site when relevant).
- Example: As a vegan recipe blogger, you might start a Facebook group for plant-based meal planning, or participate in Reddit discussions on vegan nutrition – building relationships and authority with your target audience.

By implementing these off-page SEO strategies consistently and authentically, you'll start to see your website's authority and search rankings climb – and your organic traffic and engagement soar. Of course, building high-quality backlinks takes time, effort, and a lot of patience – but the payoff is more than worth it in the long run.

Remember, off-page SEO is all about building relationships and providing value – not just to search engines, but to real people and communities. So focus on creating amazing content, connecting with others in your niche, and being a genuinely helpful and authoritative resource – and the backlinks and search success will follow naturally.

So, get out there and start building those backlinks, my friend! The world needs your expertise and insights – and with a little off-page SEO magic, you'll be unstoppable.

Chapter 5
Creating Compelling Content for Your Website

Identifying Your Target Audience and Their Pain Points

Welcome back, my content-creating comrade! Now that you've mastered the ins and outs of SEO, it's time to dive into the heart and soul of your website: your content. Because let's face it – you could have the most beautifully designed site and the most brilliant SEO strategy in the world, but if your content falls flat, none of it will matter. Your content is what will attract, engage, and convert your dream customers – and keep them coming back for more.

But before you start cranking out blog posts and videos willy-nilly, there's one crucial step you need to take: identifying your target audience and their pain points. Because when you truly understand who you're creating content for – and what keeps them up at night – you can craft messages that resonate on a deep, emotional level. And that's when the magic happens.

So, let's break down the process of getting inside your audience's heads and hearts – and using those insights to create content they can't resist!

1. **Create Detailed Buyer Personas**
   - Buyer personas are fictional representations of your ideal customers – based on real data and research about their demographics, behaviors, goals, and challenges.

- By creating detailed buyer personas, you can get a clear picture of who you're creating content for – and tailor your messaging and topics to their specific needs and interests.
- Start by gathering data on your current customers or email subscribers – like their age, location, job title, and how they found your website.
- Then, dig deeper by conducting surveys, interviews, or focus groups to uncover their biggest pain points, aspirations, and content preferences.
- Example: As a vegan recipe blogger, one of your buyer personas might be "Health-Conscious Hannah" – a 35-year-old working mom who wants to feed her family nutritious, plant-based meals but struggles with finding the time and inspiration to cook.

2. Identify Their Pain Points and Challenges

- Once you have a clear picture of your target audience, the next step is to identify the specific pain points and challenges they face – related to your niche or industry.
- These could be practical challenges (like lack of time or resources), emotional challenges (like feeling overwhelmed or unsupported), or aspirational challenges (like wanting to live a healthier or more fulfilling life).
- By understanding your audience's biggest struggles and frustrations, you can create content that offers solutions, support, and inspiration – and positions your brand as a trusted resource and ally.
- Use social listening tools, customer feedback, and industry research to uncover the most pressing pain points and challenges in your niche.

- Example: For "Health-Conscious Hannah", some key pain points might be lack of time for meal planning and prep, picky eaters in the family, and feeling uninspired by the same old recipes.

3. Map Out Their Buyer's Journey
- The buyer's journey is the path your ideal customer takes from first becoming aware of their problem or need, to considering potential solutions, to ultimately making a purchase or taking action.
- By mapping out the typical buyer's journey for your target audience, you can create content that meets them where they are – and guides them towards a decision or action.
- Consider the different stages of the buyer's journey (Awareness, Consideration, Decision) – and brainstorm content ideas that address the specific questions, concerns, and needs at each stage.
- Use a variety of content formats (blog posts, videos, ebooks, webinars, etc.) to appeal to different learning styles and preferences.
- Example: For "Health-Conscious Hannah", content at the Awareness stage might include a blog post on "10 Surprising Benefits of a Plant-Based Diet", while content at the Consideration stage might be a free meal planning guide or grocery list template.

4. Prioritize Helpfulness and Value
- At the end of the day, the most compelling content is content that is genuinely helpful and valuable to your target audience.

- Rather than just pushing your products or services, focus on creating content that educates, inspires, and empowers your readers to solve their problems and achieve their goals.
- Ask yourself with every piece of content: "How will this help my ideal customer? What will they learn or gain from consuming this?"
- Be generous with your knowledge and expertise – and don't be afraid to give away your best tips and strategies for free. The more value you provide upfront, the more trust and loyalty you'll build over time.
- Example: For "Health-Conscious Hannah", you might create a series of free video tutorials on how to meal prep vegan lunches for the week, or a downloadable cheat sheet with your top 10 time-saving kitchen hacks.

By taking the time to truly understand your target audience – and crafting content that speaks directly to their needs, challenges, and desires – you'll be able to build a loyal, engaged community of fans and customers who can't wait to devour your every word.

Remember, your content is not about you – it's about your audience. So put yourself in their shoes, listen to their feedback and questions, and always strive to create content that makes their lives better in some way. When you do that consistently and authentically, the rest (traffic, leads, sales) will follow naturally.

So, get out there and start creating, my friend! Your audience is waiting for your unique voice and perspective – and with a little empathy and elbow grease, you'll be unstoppable.

Developing a Content Strategy and Editorial Calendar

Welcome back, my content-savvy friend! Now that you've got a deep understanding of your target audience and their pain points, it's time to put that knowledge into action with a solid content strategy and editorial calendar. Because let's be real – creating compelling content is not a one-and-done kind of deal. It's an ongoing, strategic process that requires planning, consistency, and a whole lot of creativity.

But fear not – with a well-crafted content strategy and editorial calendar, you'll be able to stay organized, focused, and inspired as you create content that resonates with your audience and drives real results for your business.

So, let's dive into the nuts and bolts of developing a content strategy and editorial calendar that will keep your content engine running like a well-oiled machine!

1. Define Your Content Goals and KPIs
- Before you start creating any content, you need to know what you're trying to achieve – and how you'll measure success.
- Your content goals should be specific, measurable, achievable, relevant, and time-bound (SMART) – and tied to your overall business objectives.
- Some common content goals might include increasing brand awareness, driving traffic to your website, generating leads or sales, or building community and engagement.

- For each goal, identify the key performance indicators (KPIs) you'll use to track progress – like website traffic, social shares, email sign-ups, or revenue.
- Example: As a vegan recipe blogger, one of your content goals might be to increase email sign-ups by 25% over the next quarter – with a KPI of 100 new subscribers per month.

2. Conduct a Content Audit
- Before you start creating new content, it's important to take stock of what you already have – and how it's performing.
- Conduct a content audit of your existing blog posts, videos, social media updates, and other content assets.
- Analyze each piece of content for metrics like traffic, engagement, and conversions – as well as qualitative factors like relevance, quality, and alignment with your brand voice and values.
- Look for patterns and insights – like which topics or formats perform best, which content is outdated or irrelevant, and where there are gaps or opportunities for new content.
- Use your findings to inform your content strategy and prioritize your content creation efforts.
- Example: Your content audit might reveal that your top-performing blog posts are all related to "easy vegan desserts" – so you might plan to create more content around that theme in the future.

3. Brainstorm Content Ideas and Themes

- With your content goals and audit insights in mind, it's time to start brainstorming ideas and themes for your upcoming content.
- Use your buyer personas and keyword research to identify topics and questions that your target audience is searching for and interested in.
- Consider a mix of content formats and types – like blog posts, videos, podcasts, infographics, ebooks, and more – to appeal to different learning styles and preferences.
- Organize your ideas into themes or pillars that align with your brand and expertise – like "vegan meal prep", "plant-based nutrition", or "sustainable living".
- Create a master list of content ideas and topics that you can draw from and refine over time.
- Example: Some content ideas for your vegan recipe blog might include "10 Easy Vegan Breakfast Ideas", "The Ultimate Guide to Plant-Based Protein Sources", or "How to Transition to a Vegan Diet in 30 Days".

4. Create an Editorial Calendar

- Once you have a solid list of content ideas and themes, it's time to get organized with an editorial calendar.
- An editorial calendar is a schedule or roadmap for your content creation and publishing – typically broken down by month, week, or even day.
- Your editorial calendar should include key details like the topic or title of each piece of content, the format or type, the author or creator, the publish date, and any relevant notes or resources.

- Use a tool like Google Calendar, Trello, or Asana to create and manage your editorial calendar – and share it with your team or collaborators for transparency and accountability.
- Be sure to leave some flexibility in your calendar for timely or trending topics that may come up – but try to stick to your schedule as much as possible for consistency and momentum.
- Example: Your editorial calendar for the next month might include a weekly blog post (published every Tuesday), a bi-weekly video tutorial (published every other Thursday), and daily social media updates (Monday through Friday).

5. Establish a Content Creation Process

- Finally, to ensure that your content strategy and editorial calendar are executed effectively, you need to establish a clear and efficient content creation process.
- Break down each piece of content into smaller tasks and assignments – like research, outlining, drafting, editing, design, and promotion.
- Assign roles and responsibilities to your team members or collaborators – and set realistic deadlines and expectations for each task.
- Use project management tools, templates, and checklists to streamline your workflow and ensure consistency and quality across all your content.
- Build in time for review, feedback, and iteration – and don't be afraid to make changes or pivot your strategy based on data and insights.

- Example: Your content creation process for a blog post might include keyword research (1 hour), outlining (30 minutes), drafting (2 hours), editing (1 hour), design (30 minutes), and promotion (1 hour) – with a total timeline of 2-3 days from start to finish.

By developing a comprehensive content strategy and editorial calendar – and following a structured, streamlined content creation process – you'll be able to produce a steady stream of high-quality, audience-focused content that drives real results for your business.

Remember, your content strategy is not a static document – it's a living, breathing roadmap that should evolve and adapt over time based on your goals, your audience, and your insights. So be willing to experiment, take risks, and learn from your successes and failures along the way.

The key is to stay focused on your ultimate goal – creating content that genuinely helps and inspires your target audience – and trusting that the rest will fall into place.

So, get out there and start strategizing, my friend! Your audience is waiting for your next masterpiece – and with a little planning and perseverance, you'll be unstoppable.

Writing Engaging Blog Posts and Articles

Hello again, my wordsmithing wizard! Are you ready to take your content creation skills to the next level? Because today, we're diving deep into the art and science of writing engaging blog posts and articles that will captivate your audience and keep them coming back for more.

Whether you're a seasoned scribe or a newbie blogger, crafting compelling content is essential for building your brand, establishing your expertise, and driving traffic and engagement to your website. But with millions of blog posts and articles published every day, how can you make yours stand out from the crowd?

Fear not – with a few key strategies and techniques, you can write blog posts and articles that are not only informative and valuable, but also irresistibly engaging and shareable.

So, let's break down the anatomy of an engaging blog post or article – and explore some tips and tricks for making your content shine!

1. Start with a Strong Headline
- Your headline is the first (and sometimes only) thing that your potential reader will see – so it needs to be attention-grabbing, compelling, and irresistible.
- A great headline should be clear, specific, and benefit-driven – it should communicate the main topic or takeaway of your post, while also piquing the reader's curiosity or promising a solution to their problem.

- Use strong, active language and power words that evoke emotion or urgency – like "amazing", "proven", "secret", or "now".
- Keep your headlines relatively short and punchy – aim for around 60 characters or less for optimal readability and search engine optimization.
- Example: Instead of a generic headline like "How to Make Vegan Cookies", try something more specific and compelling like "The Secret to Perfectly Chewy Vegan Chocolate Chip Cookies (Recipe Inside!)"

2. Hook Your Reader with a Strong Introduction

- Once you've caught your reader's attention with your headline, you need to keep them engaged with a strong, compelling introduction.
- Your introduction should do three things: 1) establish the main topic or problem that your post will address, 2) promise a clear benefit or solution for the reader, and 3) entice them to keep reading.
- Use your introduction to build rapport and trust with your reader – show that you understand their pain points, struggles, or goals, and that you have the expertise or experience to help them.
- Keep your introduction relatively short and to-the-point – aim for around 100-150 words that quickly get to the meat of your post.
- Example: For a blog post on "The Secret to Perfectly Chewy Vegan Chocolate Chip Cookies", your introduction might start with a relatable problem ("Tired of vegan cookies that are dry, crumbly, or just plain blah?"), promise a solution ("Well, I've cracked the code for perfectly chewy,

gooey, mouthwatering vegan chocolate chip cookies – and I'm sharing my secrets with you today!"), and entice the reader to keep reading ("Trust me, your taste buds (and your non-vegan friends) will thank you. ").

3. Organize Your Content with Clear Subheadings

- Once you've hooked your reader with your introduction, you need to keep them engaged and oriented throughout your post with clear, logical subheadings.
- Subheadings break up your content into smaller, more digestible sections – making it easier for readers to scan, skim, and find the information they're looking for.
- Use descriptive, keyword-rich subheadings that clearly communicate the main topic or takeaway of each section – like "The Key Ingredients for Chewy Vegan Cookies" or "3 Tips for Perfectly Baked Cookies Every Time".
- Keep your subheadings relatively short and punchy – aim for around 60 characters or less for optimal readability and search engine optimization.
- Example: For a blog post on "The Secret to Perfectly Chewy Vegan Chocolate Chip Cookies", your subheadings might include "The Key Ingredients", "The Perfect Cookie Dough Consistency", "The Ideal Baking Temperature and Time", and "3 Tips for Perfectly Chewy Cookies Every Time".

4. Use Engaging, Conversational Language
- To keep your readers engaged and invested in your content, you need to write in a way that feels like a natural, friendly conversation.
- Use a warm, personal tone that speaks directly to your reader – as if you're chatting with a friend over coffee.
- Use simple, clear language that's easy to understand – avoid jargon, buzzwords, or overly complex sentence structures.
- Use plenty of examples, analogies, and stories to illustrate your points and make your content more relatable and memorable.
- Don't be afraid to inject your own personality, humor, and style into your writing – let your unique voice shine through!

Example: Instead of a formal, academic sentence like "The key to achieving the optimal texture in vegan chocolate chip cookies is to utilize a combination of plant-based fats and proteins", try something more conversational and relatable like "Want to know the secret to chewy, gooey vegan chocolate chip cookies? It's all about finding the right balance of plant-based fats (like coconut oil or vegan butter) and proteins (like almond flour or chickpea flour) to mimic the texture of traditional cookies. It might take a little experimentation, but trust me – the results are worth it! "

5. End with a Strong Conclusion and Call-to-Action
- Finally, to leave a lasting impression on your reader and encourage them to take action, you need to end your blog post or article with a strong, compelling conclusion and call-to-action.

- Your conclusion should summarize the main points or takeaways of your post, reinforce the benefits or value for the reader, and leave them feeling inspired, empowered, or motivated to act.
- Your call-to-action should be a clear, specific, and actionable request for the reader to do something – like leaving a comment, sharing your post on social media, signing up for your email list, or trying out your recipe or tip for themselves.
- Keep your conclusion and call-to-action relatively short and to-the-point – aim for around 100-150 words that pack a punch and leave a lasting impact.
- Example: For a blog post on "The Secret to Perfectly Chewy Vegan Chocolate Chip Cookies", your conclusion and call-to-action might look something like this:
- "So there you have it – the secret to perfectly chewy, gooey, mouthwatering vegan chocolate chip cookies! By using the right combination of plant-based ingredients, achieving the perfect cookie dough consistency, and baking at the ideal temperature and time, you can create cookies that will impress even the most die-hard dairy lovers.
- But don't just take my word for it – try out this recipe for yourself and let me know how it goes! Leave a comment below with your favorite vegan cookie recipe or tip, and feel free to share this post with your friends and family who are always on the hunt for the perfect vegan treat.

And if you want more delicious vegan recipes, baking tips, and kitchen hacks delivered straight to your inbox, be sure to sign up for my email newsletter (link in bio) – I promise, your taste buds will thank you! Happy baking, my friend! "

By following these strategies and techniques for writing engaging blog posts and articles, you'll be well on your way to creating content that not only informs and educates your audience but also entertains, inspires, and delights them. And when you do that consistently and authentically, you'll build a loyal, engaged community of readers who trust you, value your expertise, and can't wait to devour your next post.

Remember, writing is a skill that takes time, practice, and patience to master – so don't get discouraged if your first few posts don't feel "perfect". The key is to keep showing up, keeping learning and experimenting, and trusting in the unique voice and perspective that only you can bring to the table.

So, get out there and start writing, my friend! Your audience is waiting to be wowed by your words – and with a little creativity and heart, you'll be unstoppable.

Incorporating Multimedia Content (Videos, Podcasts, Infographics)

Welcome back, my multimedia maven! Are you ready to take your content creation game to the next level? Because today, we're diving into the world of multimedia content – and exploring how you can use videos, podcasts, infographics, and more to enhance your blog posts and articles and create a more engaging, immersive experience for your audience.

In today's digital landscape, text-based content is just the tip of the iceberg. With the rise of social media, mobile devices, and short attention spans, more and more people are craving content that's not just informative, but also entertaining, interactive, and visually appealing. That's where multimedia content comes in.

By incorporating videos, podcasts, infographics, and other multimedia elements into your blog posts and articles, you can:

- Engage multiple senses and learning styles (visual, auditory, kinesthetic)
- Break up long blocks of text and make your content more scannable and digestible
- Illustrate complex ideas or processes in a more clear, concise, and compelling way
- Showcase your personality, expertise, and brand voice in a more dynamic, authentic way
- Increase your content's shareability, virality, and overall impact and reach

But with so many multimedia options to choose from, where do you start? And how do you ensure that your multimedia content is not just flashy, but also strategic, purposeful, and aligned with your overall content goals and audience needs?

Fear not – we've got you covered! Let's break down some of the most popular types of multimedia content, along with some tips and best practices for incorporating them into your blog posts and articles.

1. Videos
- Videos are one of the most powerful and engaging types of multimedia content – they allow you to combine visuals, audio, and motion to tell a story, convey a message, or demonstrate a process in a way that text alone simply can't.
- There are many different types of videos you can create for your blog posts and articles, such as:
- Explainer videos that break down a complex topic or concept in a simple, easy-to-understand way
- How-to videos that walk viewers through a specific process or tutorial step-by-step
- Interview videos that feature you or an expert in your niche sharing insights, advice, or personal stories
- Behind-the-scenes videos that give viewers a peek into your brand, business, or creative process
- Animated videos that use illustrations, graphics, and voiceover to convey a message or story in a fun, engaging way

When creating videos for your blog posts and articles, keep these tips in mind:
- Keep your videos relatively short and to-the-point – aim for 1-3 minutes for most types of videos (with the exception of longer-form content like webinars or interviews)
- Use a clear, concise script or outline to keep your video focused and on-topic
- Invest in decent equipment (camera, microphone, lighting) and editing software to ensure high-quality production value
- Optimize your videos for search engines by including relevant keywords in your video title, description, and tags
- Embed your videos directly into your blog post or article, and consider also uploading them to video-sharing platforms like YouTube or Vimeo for added exposure and reach

2. Podcasts
- Podcasts are another great way to add a new dimension to your blog posts and articles – they allow you to share your expertise, insights, and personality in a more intimate, conversational way that can build deeper connections with your audience.
- There are many different formats and styles of podcasts you can create for your blog posts and articles, such as:
- Solo podcasts where you share your thoughts, experiences, or advice on a particular topic or theme
- Interview podcasts where you have conversations with experts, influencers, or thought leaders in your niche

- Roundtable podcasts where you bring together a group of people to discuss or debate a particular topic or issue
- Storytelling podcasts where you use narrative techniques to weave a compelling story or message
- When creating podcasts for your blog posts and articles, keep these tips in mind:
- Invest in decent equipment (microphone, recording software) to ensure high-quality audio production
- Plan and prepare your podcast content in advance, with a clear structure, flow, and call-to-action
- Edit your podcast for clarity, concision, and pacing – aim for 20-30 minutes for most types of podcasts (with the exception of longer-form content like interviews or storytelling)
- Optimize your podcasts for search engines by including relevant keywords in your podcast title, description, and tags
- Embed your podcasts directly into your blog post or article using a podcast player or embed code, and consider also submitting them to podcast directories like Apple Podcasts or Spotify for added exposure and reach

3. Infographics
- Infographics are a powerful way to visually communicate complex data, statistics, or processes in a way that's easy to understand and remember – they combine text, images, and design elements to create a compelling, shareable piece of content.

There are many different types of infographics you can create for your blog posts and articles, such as:
- Statistical infographics that use charts, graphs, and other data visualizations to illustrate trends, patterns, or comparisons
- Process infographics that use flowcharts, timelines, or step-by-step diagrams to explain a sequence of events or actions
- Geographic infographics that use maps, icons, and other visual elements to represent location-based data or information
- Comparison infographics that use side-by-side or overlapping visuals to highlight the similarities or differences between two or more topics or entities
- When creating infographics for your blog posts and articles, keep these tips in mind:
- Use a clear, consistent design style that aligns with your brand colors, fonts, and overall aesthetic
- Keep your infographics relatively simple and focused – aim for 5-10 key data points or takeaways per infographic
- Use high-quality, relevant images and icons to illustrate your points and break up the text
- Cite your sources and data references to ensure accuracy and credibility
- Optimize your infographics for search engines by including relevant keywords in your infographic title, description, and alt text
- Embed your infographics directly into your blog post or article, and consider also sharing them on social media or infographic directories like Visual.ly or Infographic Journal for added exposure and reach

By incorporating these and other types of multimedia content into your blog posts and articles, you can create a more dynamic, engaging, and memorable experience for your audience – one that not only informs and educates them but also entertains and inspires them.

Remember, the key to effective multimedia content is to use it strategically and purposefully – not just for the sake of having it, but for the sake of enhancing your message, supporting your content goals, and delivering real value to your audience.

So, get out there and start experimenting with different types of multimedia content – and see how it can transform your blog posts and articles from good to great!

Repurposing and Updating Your Content

Welcome back, my content creation connoisseur! Are you ready to take your content strategy to the next level? Because today, we're talking about one of the most powerful yet often overlooked aspects of content creation: repurposing and updating your existing content.

As a busy blogger, marketer, or business owner, you probably spend a lot of time and effort creating new content – whether it's blog posts, articles, videos, podcasts, or infographics. But what happens to that content once it's published? Does it just sit there on your website or social media feed, collecting virtual dust?

If so, you're missing out on a huge opportunity to get more mileage out of your content – and reach new audiences, boost your search engine rankings, and drive more traffic and engagement to your website. That's where repurposing and updating your content comes in.

By repurposing your existing content into different formats, updating it for relevance and accuracy, and promoting it to new channels and audiences, you can:

- Save time and effort on content creation (while still delivering value to your audience)
- Reach new people who may prefer different formats or platforms
- Improve your search engine rankings (by providing fresh, relevant content on a consistent basis)
- Drive more traffic, engagement, and conversions to your website

- Establish yourself as a trusted, authoritative source in your niche or industry

But how exactly do you go about repurposing and updating your content? And what are some specific strategies and best practices you can use to maximize the impact and reach of your repurposed content?

Fear not – we've got you covered! Let's break down some of the most effective ways to repurpose and update your content, along with some tips and examples to help you get started.

1. Turn Blog Posts into Videos or Podcasts
- One of the easiest ways to repurpose your blog posts or articles is to turn them into videos or podcasts – this allows you to reach new audiences who may prefer audio or visual content over text.
- To turn a blog post into a video, you can:
- Create a slideshow or screen recording of the post, with voiceover narration or text overlays
- Film yourself or someone else summarizing the key points of the post, using visual aids or examples
- Animate the post using graphics, illustrations, or whiteboard drawings
- To turn a blog post into a podcast, you can:
- Record yourself or someone else reading the post aloud, with additional commentary or insights
- Interview an expert or thought leader on the topic of the post, using the post as a starting point for discussion
- Create a panel discussion or roundtable on the topic of the post, with multiple guests or co-hosts

- When repurposing your blog posts into videos or podcasts, keep these tips in mind:
- Keep the content concise and focused – aim for 5-10 minutes for videos and 20-30 minutes for podcasts
- Use engaging visuals, music, or sound effects to keep viewers or listeners interested and engaged
- Include a clear call-to-action at the end of the video or podcast, directing viewers or listeners back to your website or other content
- Optimize the video or podcast for search engines, using relevant keywords and tags in the title, description, and metadata

2. Create Infographics or SlideShares from Blog Posts

- Another great way to repurpose your blog posts or articles is to turn them into infographics or SlideShares – this allows you to present the information in a more visual, scannable, and shareable format.
- To create an infographic from a blog post, you can:
- Identify the key data points, statistics, or takeaways from the post
- Use a tool like Canva, Venngage, or Piktochart to create a visual layout for the infographic
- Add images, icons, and other design elements to make the infographic more engaging and memorable
- To create a SlideShare from a blog post, you can:
- Break down the post into key sections or talking points
- Use a tool like PowerPoint, Keynote, or Google Slides to create a slide deck for each section
- Add images, graphs, and other visual aids to illustrate your points and keep readers engaged

- When creating infographics or SlideShares from your blog posts, keep these tips in mind:
- Keep the content focused and visually appealing – aim for 5-10 key points or takeaways per infographic or SlideShare
- Use a consistent color scheme, font, and design style that aligns with your brand
- Include your website URL, logo, and social media handles on the infographic or SlideShare for branding and attribution
- Share the infographic or SlideShare on social media, SlideShare.net, and other relevant platforms for added exposure and reach

3. Update and Refresh Older Blog Posts
- In addition to repurposing your content into new formats, it's also important to regularly update and refresh your older blog posts or articles – this helps to ensure that your content stays relevant, accurate, and up-to-date over time.
- To update and refresh an older blog post, you can:
- Check for any outdated information, statistics, or examples and update them with newer, more relevant data
- Add new sections, tips, or insights that you've learned since originally publishing the post
- Improve the formatting, layout, and visual design of the post to make it more engaging and user-friendly
- Optimize the post for search engines, using relevant keywords and meta tags in the title, headings, and body copy

- When updating and refreshing your older blog posts, keep these tips in mind:
- Focus on your most popular and evergreen posts first – these are the ones that are most likely to drive traffic and engagement over time
- Use Google Analytics or other web analytics tools to identify posts that have high bounce rates, low time on page, or other engagement metrics that could be improved
- Include an "Updated on [date]" note at the top of the post to let readers know that the content has been refreshed and is still relevant
- Share the updated post on social media and other relevant platforms to drive new traffic and engagement to the post

By repurposing and updating your content on a regular basis, you can get more value and impact out of every piece of content you create – and build a stronger, more sustainable content strategy over time.

Remember, the key to effective content repurposing and updating is to stay focused on your audience's needs and preferences – and to always strive to deliver the most relevant, valuable, and engaging content possible, no matter what format or platform you're using.

So, get out there and start breathing new life into your old content – and watch as your traffic, engagement, and conversions soar to new heights!

Chapter 6
Leveraging Social Media for Business Growth

Choosing the Right Social Media Platforms for Your Business

Hey there, social media superstar! Are you ready to take your online business to the next level? Because today, we're diving into the world of social media – and exploring how you can leverage the power of platforms like Facebook, Instagram, Twitter, and LinkedIn to grow your brand, reach new audiences, and drive more traffic and sales to your website.

In today's digital age, social media is no longer just a nice-to-have – it's a must-have for any business that wants to succeed online. With over 3.6 billion people using social media worldwide (and counting), it's one of the most powerful and cost-effective ways to connect with your target audience, build relationships, and promote your products or services.

But with so many social media platforms to choose from – each with its own unique features, demographics, and best practices – it can be overwhelming to know where to start. Should you be on Facebook, Instagram, Twitter, LinkedIn, TikTok, Pinterest, YouTube, or all of the above? And how do you create a social media strategy that aligns with your business goals, brand voice, and audience preferences?

Fear not – we've got you covered! Let's break down the process of choosing the right social media platforms for your business, along with some tips and best practices for creating a winning social media strategy.

1. Define Your Social Media Goals
Before you start creating accounts on every social media platform under the sun, it's important to take a step back and define your goals for social media.

What do you want to achieve through social media? Some common goals might include:
- Increasing brand awareness and reach
- Driving traffic to your website or blog
- Generating leads or sales for your products or services
- Building relationships and engaging with your audience
- Establishing your brand as a thought leader or authority in your niche
- Your goals will help guide your decision on which social media platforms to focus on, as well as what types of content and strategies to use.

For example, if your main goal is to drive traffic to your website, you might focus on platforms like Facebook and Twitter that allow you to share links and drive clicks. If your goal is to showcase your products or services visually, you might prioritize platforms like Instagram or Pinterest.

2. Research Your Target Audience
Once you've defined your social media goals, the next step is to research your target audience and identify which social media platforms they're most active on.

Think about the demographics, interests, and behaviors of your ideal customer or client:
- What age range are they in?
- What gender do they identify as?
- Where do they live?
- What are their hobbies, interests, and pain points?
- What types of content do they engage with most?

Use tools like Facebook Audience Insights, Twitter Analytics, or Instagram Insights to get more detailed data on your audience's social media habits and preferences.

Look at your competitors' social media presence as well – which platforms are they most active on, and what types of content and engagement are they getting?

Based on your research, identify the top 2-3 social media platforms where your target audience is most active and engaged.

3. Evaluate Each Platform's Features and Best Practices

Once you've identified the top social media platforms for your business, it's important to evaluate each platform's unique features, strengths, and best practices.

Here's a quick overview of some of the most popular social media platforms and their key features:

- Facebook: The largest social media platform, with over 2.7 billion monthly active users. Ideal for building brand awareness, driving traffic, and creating communities through features like pages, groups, and events.
- Instagram: A visual platform with over 1 billion monthly active users, known for its emphasis on high-quality photos and videos. Ideal for showcasing products, behind-the-scenes content, and user-generated content through features like posts, stories, and reels.

- Twitter: A fast-paced, text-based platform with over 330 million monthly active users, known for its real-time updates and conversations. Ideal for sharing news, insights, and engaging with customers through features like tweets, hashtags, and direct messages.
- LinkedIn: A professional networking platform with over 750 million members, known for its focus on B2B connections and thought leadership. Ideal for building relationships, generating leads, and establishing your brand as an authority through features like company pages, articles, and groups.

Each platform also has its own best practices and guidelines for content creation, posting frequency, and engagement. For example:

On Facebook, the algorithm prioritizes content that sparks meaningful conversations and interactions, so it's important to create posts that encourage comments, shares, and reactions.

On Instagram, the most successful posts tend to be high-quality, visually appealing photos or videos that tell a story or evoke an emotion. It's also important to use relevant hashtags and engage with your followers through comments and direct messages.

On Twitter, the key is to be concise, timely, and engaging – tweets with images or videos tend to perform best, and it's important to use hashtags and mentions to join relevant conversations and reach new audiences.

By understanding each platform's unique features and best practices, you can create a social media strategy that maximizes your presence and impact on each platform.

4. Create a Content Strategy and Posting Schedule

Once you've chosen your social media platforms and evaluated their best practices, it's time to create a content strategy and posting schedule that aligns with your goals and audience preferences.

Your content strategy should include:

- The types of content you'll create and share on each platform (e.g. blog posts, photos, videos, infographics, etc.)
- The topics and themes you'll cover, based on your audience's interests and pain pointsThe tone and voice you'll use, based on your brand personality and values
- The posting frequency and timing for each platform, based on when your audience is most active and engaged
- Use a content calendar or scheduling tool like Hootsuite, Buffer, or Sprout Social to plan and organize your posts in advance.
- Aim for a mix of content types and formats, including:
- Educational or informative content that provides value to your audience
- Entertaining or inspiring content that evokes an emotional response
- Promotional content that showcases your products or services (but don't overdo it – aim for a ratio of 80% valuable content to 20% promotional content)
- User-generated content or customer spotlights that build social proof and engagement
- Don't forget to also plan for timely or trending content that relates to your niche or industry – this can help you join relevant conversations and reach new audiences.

5. Engage and Interact with Your Audience

- Finally, one of the most important aspects of a successful social media strategy is engagement and interaction with your audience.
- Social media is a two-way conversation – it's not just about broadcasting your own content, but also about listening to and engaging with your followers.
- Make a habit of regularly checking your social media accounts and responding to comments, questions, and messages in a timely and authentic way.
- Use social media listening tools like Hootsuite Insights or Sprout Social to monitor mentions of your brand or relevant keywords, and join conversations where appropriate.
- Encourage your followers to engage with your content by asking questions, running polls or contests, or creating user-generated content campaigns.
- Collaborate with other brands, influencers, or thought leaders in your niche to cross-promote content and reach new audiences.
- By consistently engaging and interacting with your audience, you'll build stronger relationships, increase brand loyalty, and create a community of advocates and fans who will help spread the word about your business.

Choosing the right social media platforms and creating a winning social media strategy takes time, effort, and experimentation – but the payoff is well worth it. By leveraging the power of social media to connect with your target audience, promote your brand, and drive traffic and sales to your website, you'll be well on your way to online business success.

Remember, social media is always evolving – new platforms, features, and trends are emerging all the time. The key is to stay flexible, adaptable, and willing to experiment with new ideas and approaches. Don't be afraid to try new things, measure your results, and adjust your strategy as needed.

So, get out there and start building your social media empire – your audience is waiting to connect with you!

Creating a Social Media Strategy and Content Plan

Welcome back, social media maverick! Now that you've chosen the right social media platforms for your business and identified your target audience, it's time to dive into the nitty-gritty of creating a killer social media strategy and content plan. Because let's face it – without a clear strategy and plan, your social media efforts will be about as effective as a screen door on a submarine.

But fear not – with a little bit of planning, creativity, and elbow grease, you can create a social media strategy and content plan that will help you achieve your business goals, engage your audience, and stand out from the crowd.

So, what exactly is a social media strategy and content plan, and how do you create one? Let's break it down:

1. Define Your Social Media Goals and Objectives
- Your social media strategy should start with a clear understanding of what you want to achieve through social media.
- Do you want to increase brand awareness, drive website traffic, generate leads, boost engagement, or something else entirely?
- Your goals should be specific, measurable, achievable, relevant, and time-bound (SMART) – for example, "Increase website traffic from social media by 25% in the next 3 months."
- Your objectives should support your overall business goals and be aligned with your target audience's needs and interests.

2. Conduct a Social Media Audit
- Before you start creating new content, it's important to take stock of your existing social media presence and performance.
- Conduct a social media audit to evaluate your current profiles, followers, engagement rates, and top-performing content.
- Use tools like Hootsuite Insights, Sprout Social, or native analytics on each platform to gather data and insights.
- Look for patterns, trends, and opportunities for improvement – for example, if your Instagram posts with user-generated content get the most engagement, you might want to incorporate more of that into your strategy.

3. Develop Your Brand Voice and Tone
- Your social media content should reflect your brand's unique personality, values, and voice.
- Develop a clear and consistent brand voice and tone that resonates with your target audience and sets you apart from competitors.
- Consider factors like your brand's mission, values, and unique selling proposition (USP) – for example, if your brand is all about sustainability and eco-friendliness, your social media content should reflect that.
- Create a brand style guide that outlines your brand voice, tone, and visual identity (colors, fonts, imagery) to ensure consistency across all your social media content.

4. Plan Your Content Mix
- Now it's time to plan out the types of content you'll create and share on each social media platform.
- Your content mix should include a variety of formats, topics, and purposes that align with your goals and audience preferences.
- Some common types of social media content include:
- Educational or informative content (blog posts, tutorials, tips)
- Entertaining or inspiring content (memes, quotes, behind-the-scenes photos)
- Promotional content (product launches, sales, special offers)
- User-generated content (customer reviews, photos, testimonials)
- Curated content (articles, videos, or posts from other sources that are relevant to your niche)
- Aim for a balance of content types that provide value to your audience while also promoting your brand and products/services.

5. Create a Content Calendar
To stay organized and consistent with your social media posting, create a content calendar that maps out your content for the coming weeks or months.

Your content calendar should include:
- The date and time of each post
- The social media platform(s) you'll be posting on
- The type of content (blog post, photo, video, etc.
- The topic or theme of the content
- Any relevant links, hashtags, or calls-to-action (CTAs)

- Use a tool like Google Sheets, Trello, or Hootsuite to create and manage your content calendar.
- Be sure to leave some flexibility in your calendar for timely or trending content that may come up – for example, if there's a major news event or holiday that's relevant to your niche, you may want to create content around that.

6. Optimize Your Content for Each Platform
- Each social media platform has its own unique features, algorithms, and best practices for content optimization.
- To maximize your reach and engagement on each platform, be sure to optimize your content accordingly.
- Some tips for optimizing your social media content:
- Use high-quality, eye-catching visuals (photos, videos, graphics) that stand out in the feed
- Write compelling, keyword-rich captions that grab attention and encourage engagement
- Use relevant hashtags to increase discoverability and reach new audiences
- Tag relevant users or brands in your posts to encourage shares and collaborations
- Include a clear and compelling call-to-action (CTA) in each post, such as "click the link in bio to read more" or "tag a friend who needs to see this"
- Stay up-to-date on the latest features and best practices for each platform, and adjust your strategy accordingly.

7. Measure and Analyze Your Results

Finally, to ensure that your social media strategy is working and driving real results for your business, it's important to regularly measure and analyze your performance.

Use tools like Google Analytics, Hootsuite Insights, or native analytics on each platform to track key metrics like:

- Reach and impressions (how many people are seeing your content)
- Engagement rate (likes, comments, shares, clicks)
- Website traffic and conversions from social media
- Follower growth and demographics
- Look for patterns and insights in your data – for example, if certain types of content or posting times are driving the most engagement, double down on those in your strategy.
- Use your insights to continually refine and optimize your social media strategy over time – don't be afraid to experiment with new ideas and approaches to see what works best for your unique audience and goals.

Creating a social media strategy and content plan may seem like a lot of work upfront – but trust me, it's worth it. By taking the time to plan and optimize your social media presence, you'll be able to build a loyal and engaged following, drive meaningful results for your business, and have a lot more fun in the process.

Remember, social media is all about building relationships and providing value to your audience. So focus on creating content that educates, entertains, and inspires – and the rest will follow.

Growing Your Followers and Engagement

Hey there, social media superstar! So you've got your social media strategy and content plan in place – now it's time to focus on growing your followers and engagement. Because let's be real – without an engaged and loyal following, your social media efforts will be about as effective as a chocolate teapot.

But don't worry – with a little bit of creativity, consistency, and hustle, you can attract and retain a thriving community of followers who love your brand and can't wait to engage with your content.

So, what exactly is social media engagement, and how do you get more of it? Let's dive in:

1. Understand the Importance of Engagement
- Social media engagement refers to the interactions and actions that your followers take on your posts – things like likes, comments, shares, clicks, and saves.
- Engagement is important because it's a key indicator of how well your content is resonating with your audience – and it's also a major factor in how social media algorithms prioritize and distribute your content.
- The more engagement your posts get, the more likely they are to be seen by a wider audience – both among your existing followers and potential new followers who discover your content through their feeds or search results.

- Engagement also helps to build trust, loyalty, and relationships with your followers – when they interact with your brand on social media, they feel more connected and invested in your success.

2. Create Engaging and Shareable Content

The foundation of growing your followers and engagement is creating high-quality, valuable content that your audience can't resist interacting with.

Focus on creating content that is:
- Relevant and useful to your target audience's needs, interests, and pain points
- Visually appealing and eye-catching – use high-quality photos, videos, and graphics that stand out in the feed
- Emotionally compelling – evoke feelings of joy, inspiration, nostalgia, or humor that encourage people to react and share
- Timely and topical – tap into current events, trends, or seasonal themes that are top-of-mind for your audience
- Interactive and participatory – ask questions, run polls, or create challenges that encourage people to comment and engage
- Experiment with different types of content formats and topics to see what resonates best with your unique audience – and don't be afraid to think outside the box and try something new.

3. Use Hashtags Strategically
- Hashtags are a powerful tool for increasing the discoverability and reach of your social media content.

- When you include relevant hashtags in your posts, you make it easier for people who are interested in those topics to find and engage with your content – even if they don't already follow your account.
- Research and use a mix of popular, niche, and branded hashtags that are relevant to your content and target audience.
- Popular hashtags (like #love or #instagood) can help you reach a wider audience, but they're also more competitive – niche hashtags (like #veganrecipes or #sustainablefashion) can help you reach a more targeted and engaged audience in your specific industry or topic.
- Branded hashtags (like your company name or campaign slogan) can help you build brand recognition and user-generated content – encourage your followers to use your branded hashtag when they post about your products or services.

4. Engage with Your Followers and Other Accounts

- Social media is a two-way conversation – to grow your followers and engagement, you need to be an active and engaged participant in the community.
- Make a habit of regularly responding to comments, questions, and messages from your followers – show them that you value their input and appreciate their support.
- But don't just engage with your own followers – also take the time to like, comment, and share content from other accounts in your niche or industry.

- By engaging with other accounts, you can build relationships, increase your visibility, and potentially gain new followers who discover your brand through your interactions.
- You can also use social media listening tools (like Hootsuite or Sprout Social) to monitor mentions of your brand or relevant keywords – and jump into conversations where you can add value or showcase your expertise.

5. Run Contests and Giveaways
- People love free stuff – and running contests and giveaways on social media can be a great way to boost your followers and engagement.
- Choose a prize that is relevant and valuable to your target audience – like your products, services, or gift cards.
- Create clear and simple rules for entering the contest – like following your account, liking the post, tagging friends in the comments, or using a branded hashtag.
- Promote your contest across all your social media channels and email list – and consider partnering with other brands or influencers to expand your reach.
- Be sure to follow through and announce the winner(s) publicly – and thank everyone who participated for their support and enthusiasm.

6. Collaborate with Other Brands and Influencers

Collaborating with other brands and influencers in your niche can be a powerful way to grow your followers and engagement.

Look for brands or influencers who share your values, target audience, and content style – and reach out to propose a collaboration.

Collaboration ideas could include:

- Guest posting on each other's blogs or social media channels
- Co-creating content (like a video, podcast, or e-book) together
- Running a joint contest or giveaway
- Cross-promoting each other's products or services to your respective audiences
- By collaborating with other brands and influencers, you can tap into their existing audience, build relationships, and provide value to your followers in new and exciting ways.

7. Analyze and Optimize Your Performance

- Finally, to ensure that your efforts to grow your followers and engagement are working, it's important to regularly analyze and optimize your social media performance.
- Use social media analytics tools (like those mentioned earlier) to track key metrics like follower growth, engagement rate, and website traffic from social media.
- Look for patterns and insights in your data – like which types of content, topics, or posting times are driving the most engagement and follows.

- Use this data to inform and optimize your social media strategy over time – double down on what's working, and experiment with new ideas to keep things fresh and exciting for your audience.

Growing your social media followers and engagement takes time, effort, and patience – but the payoff is so worth it. By building a loyal and engaged community around your brand, you'll not only drive more traffic, leads, and sales – but you'll also create a sense of connection, trust, and loyalty that goes way beyond the screen.

So keep showing up, keep creating amazing content, and keep engaging with your audience – and watch your social media presence (and your business) soar to new heights!

Running Social Media Ads and Promotions

Alright, social media maven – are you ready to take your strategy to the next level? Because today, we're talking about one of the most powerful tools in your social media arsenal: paid advertising.

Now, I know what you might be thinking – "But wait, I thought social media was all about organic reach and engagement!" And while that's certainly an important part of the equation, the reality is that social media algorithms are making it harder and harder for businesses to reach their ideal audience through organic content alone.

That's where social media ads and promotions come in – by investing in paid advertising, you can amplify your reach, target your ideal customers with laser precision, and drive even more traffic, leads, and sales for your business.

But with so many different ad platforms, formats, and strategies to choose from, it can be overwhelming to know where to start. Fear not – we've got you covered!

In this section, we'll break down everything you need to know about running effective social media ads and promotions – from setting your budget and goals to designing your creative and measuring your results. So grab a coffee (or a cocktail), and let's dive in!

But when done right, social media ads can help you reach new audiences, build brand awareness, drive website traffic and sales, and ultimately grow your business in ways that organic social media simply can't.

1. Set Your Advertising Budget and Goals

Before you start running any social media ads, it's important to have a clear idea of your advertising budget and goals.

Your budget will depend on factors like your overall marketing budget, the cost of advertising on your chosen platform(s), and the expected return on investment (ROI) of your ads.

As a general rule of thumb, it's a good idea to start small and test the waters before investing a large amount of money into social media advertising. You can always scale up your budget as you start seeing positive results.

Your advertising goals should be specific, measurable, achievable, relevant, and time-bound (SMART) – just like your overall social media goals. Some common goals for social media advertising include:

- Increasing brand awareness and reach
- Driving website traffic and sales
- Generating leads and email subscribers
- Boosting engagement and social proof
- Promoting specific products, services, or events

2. Choose Your Ad Platform(s) and Format(s)

Once you've set your budget and goals, it's time to choose which social media platform(s) and ad format(s) you want to use.

The most popular social media ad platforms include:

- Facebook Ads
- Instagram Ads
- Twitter Ads
- LinkedIn Ads
- Pinterest Ads

- TikTok Ads
- Each platform offers a variety of ad formats, such as:
- Image ads
- Video ads
- Carousel ads (multiple images or videos in a single ad)
- Collection ads (a group of products showcased together)
- Stories ads (full-screen, vertical ads that appear in between user stories)
- The right platform(s) and format(s) for your business will depend on factors like your target audience, ad goals, and creative assets.

For example, if you're a B2B company trying to reach decision-makers, LinkedIn Ads might be a good choice. If you're an e-commerce brand with visually stunning products, Instagram Stories Ads could be a great way to showcase them.

3. Define Your Target Audience

One of the biggest advantages of social media advertising is the ability to target your ideal customers with incredible precision.

Each ad platform offers a variety of targeting options, such as:

- Demographics (age, gender, location, etc.)
- Interests and behaviors (based on users' activity on and off the platform)
- Custom audiences (people who have already interacted with your brand, such as website visitors or email subscribers)
- Lookalike audiences (people who share similar characteristics to your existing customers or followers)

- By combining these targeting options, you can create highly specific and relevant audiences for your ads – ensuring that you're reaching the right people with the right message at the right time.

For example, if you're a local yoga studio, you could target women aged 25-45 who live within a 10-mile radius of your studio and have expressed an interest in wellness, fitness, or mindfulness on social media.

4. Create Compelling Ad Creative

Once you've defined your target audience, it's time to create ad creative that will stop them in their tracks and compel them to take action.

Your ad creative should be visually stunning, emotionally compelling, and optimized for the specific ad format and platform you're using.

Some tips for creating effective ad creative include:
- Use high-quality, eye-catching images or videos that showcase your product or service in action
- Include a clear and compelling headline that communicates your unique value proposition
- Write descriptive, benefits-focused ad copy that speaks directly to your target audience's needs and desires
- Use a strong call-to-action (CTA) that tells users exactly what you want them to do (e.g. "Shop Now", "Learn More", "Sign Up")
- Test multiple versions of your ad creative to see which performs best (known as A/B testing)
- Remember, your ad creative is often the first impression that potential customers will have of your brand – so make it count!

5. Set Up Your Ad Campaign

Now that you've got your budget, goals, target audience, and ad creative ready to go, it's time to set up your ad campaign in your chosen platform(s).

Each platform has its own ad manager or dashboard where you can create and manage your campaigns, ad sets, and individual ads.

In your ad campaign setup, you'll typically need to:
- Choose your campaign objective (e.g. brand awareness, traffic, conversions)
- Set your budget and schedule (e.g. daily or lifetime budget, start and end dates)
- Define your target audience and placement options (e.g. which devices and platforms your ads will appear on)
- Upload your ad creative and write your ad copy
- Set your billing and payment information
- Be sure to double-check all your settings and preview your ads before launching your campaign – you want to make sure everything looks and works as intended!

6. Monitor and Optimize Your Ad Performance

Once your ad campaign is up and running, it's important to regularly monitor and optimize its performance to ensure you're getting the best possible results for your budget.

Each ad platform provides detailed analytics and reporting on metrics like:
- Reach and impressions (how many people saw your ad)
- Clicks and click-through rate (CTR) (how many people clicked on your ad and how often)
- Cost per click (CPC) or cost per thousand impressions (CPM) (how much you're paying for each click or impression)

Conversion rate and cost per conversion (how many people took your desired action, such as making a purchase or signing up for your email list, and how much you paid for each conversion)

Use these metrics to identify which ads, audiences, and placements are performing well – and which ones might need some tweaking.

Some common optimization tactics include:
- Adjusting your targeting criteria to reach a more relevant or engaged audience
- Changing your ad creative or copy to better resonate with your target audience
- Increasing or decreasing your budget based on your ad performance and ROI
- Pausing or turning off underperforming ads or ad sets

Remember, social media advertising is an ongoing process of experimentation, learning, and optimization. Don't be afraid to try new things, test different approaches, and continually refine your strategy based on your results.

Social media advertising can be an incredibly powerful tool for growing your business and reaching your marketing goals – but it's not a magic bullet. It takes careful planning, creative execution, and continuous optimization to truly succeed.

Collaborating with Influencers and Other Businesses

Hey there, social media collaborator extraordinaire! Are you ready to take your social media game to the next level? Because today, we're talking about one of the most powerful strategies for growing your brand, expanding your reach, and building credibility online: collaborating with influencers and other businesses.

In today's digital landscape, collaboration is key. No brand is an island – and by partnering with other businesses and influencers in your niche, you can tap into new audiences, create amazing content, and achieve your marketing goals faster and more effectively than you ever could alone.

But what exactly does collaboration look like on social media? And how can you find the right partners, create win-win partnerships, and measure the success of your collaborative efforts?

Fear not – we've got you covered! In this section, we'll explore the ins and outs of social media collaboration, and give you all the tools and strategies you need to start building powerful partnerships that drive real results for your business.
So grab a notebook (or a Google doc), and let's dive in!

1. Understand the Benefits of Collaboration
Before we get into the nitty-gritty of how to collaborate on social media, let's take a moment to understand why collaboration is so powerful.

By collaborating with other businesses or influencers, you can:
- Reach new audiences that might not have discovered your brand otherwise
- Leverage the credibility and authority of your collaborators to build trust and credibility for your own brand
- Create fresh, engaging content that showcases your products or services in a new light
- Cross-promote your brand and offerings to your collaborator's followers, and vice versa
- Build relationships and networks within your industry or niche that can lead to future opportunities and partnerships

In short, collaboration is a win-win-win: a win for you, a win for your collaborator, and a win for your audience, who gets to discover new brands, products, and content that they'll love.

2. Identify Potential Collaborators

Now that you understand the benefits of collaboration, it's time to start identifying potential collaborators for your brand.

When looking for collaborators, consider:
- Brands or influencers that share your target audience and values, but aren't direct competitors
- Brands or influencers that have a complementary product or service to yours (e.g. a beauty brand collaborating with a fashion influencer)
- Brands or influencers that have a similar aesthetic, tone, or style to your brand

- Brands or influencers that have a strong, engaged following on the social media platforms where you want to grow your presence

You can find potential collaborators by:
- Researching hashtags, keywords, and topics related to your niche or industry on social media
- Looking at the brands or influencers that your target audience already follows and engages with
- Attending industry events, conferences, or networking groups to meet potential collaborators in person
- Reaching out to brands or influencers you admire and proposing a collaboration idea
- Remember, the key is to find collaborators who are a genuine fit for your brand and audience – not just anyone with a large following or big name recognition.

3. Propose a Win-Win Collaboration

Once you've identified some potential collaborators, it's time to reach out and propose a collaboration idea.

When proposing a collaboration, be sure to:
- Introduce yourself and your brand, and explain why you think a collaboration would be mutually beneficial
- Be specific about what kind of collaboration you're proposing (e.g. a social media takeover, a co-branded product, a joint webinar or event)
- Outline the goals and expected outcomes of the collaboration for both parties
- Provide some initial ideas or examples of what the collaboration could look like in practice
- Be open to feedback, suggestions, and modifications from your potential collaborator

Remember, the key is to propose a collaboration that is truly a win-win for both parties – not just a one-sided ask or favor.

If your potential collaborator is interested, set up a call or meeting to discuss the details further and iron out any logistical or creative questions.

4. Create Amazing Collaborative Content

Once you've agreed on a collaboration idea and hammered out the details, it's time to start creating some amazing collaborative content!

Depending on the type of collaboration you're doing, this could involve:

- Co-creating social media posts, stories, or videos that showcase both of your brands or products
- Hosting a joint social media takeover, where you and your collaborator post on each other's accounts for a day or week
- Developing a co-branded product, service, or offering that combines the best of both of your brands
- Running a joint contest, giveaway, or promotion that encourages both of your audiences to engage and participate
- Hosting a webinar, livestream, or event that features both of your expertise and insights

When creating collaborative content, be sure to:

- Align on a common aesthetic, tone, and style that represents both of your brands authentically
- Clearly communicate each party's roles, responsibilities, and deadlines throughout the content creation process
- Give each other plenty of creative freedom and trust to bring your unique perspectives and skills to the table

- Have fun and let your personalities shine through – the best collaborations are the ones that feel natural, genuine, and enjoyable for everyone involved!

5. Promote and Amplify Your Collaboration

Once you've created your amazing collaborative content, it's time to get it out into the world and start driving some serious buzz and engagement!

When promoting your collaboration, be sure to:
- Post the content on both of your social media accounts and encourage your followers to check it out and engage with it
- Use relevant hashtags, tags, and mentions to increase the visibility and reach of your collaborative content
- Share behind-the-scenes photos, videos, or stories that give your followers a peek into the collaboration process and build anticipation for the final product
- Run paid social media ads or promotions to amplify the reach of your collaborative content and drive even more traffic and engagement
- Engage with your followers' comments, questions, and feedback on the collaborative content to build relationships and show that you value their input

Remember, the key is to treat your collaboration like a major event or launch – not just a one-off post or project. The more you can build buzz and anticipation around your collaboration, the more impact and results it will likely have.

6. Measure and Analyze Your Results

Finally, once your collaboration is out in the world and generating engagement, it's important to measure and analyze the results to see what worked, what didn't, and how you can improve for next time.

Some key metrics to track for your collaboration include:
- Reach and impressions (how many people saw your collaborative content)
- Engagement rate (likes, comments, shares, saves, etc. divided by total impressions)
- Click-through rate (how many people clicked on any links or calls-to-action in your collaborative content)
- Follower growth (how many new followers each collaborator gained as a result of the collaboration)
- Sales or conversions (if applicable, how many sales or signups each collaborator generated from the collaboration)
- Use these metrics to identify what elements of your collaboration resonated most with your audience, and what you might want to tweak or improve for future collaborations.
- Be sure to also gather qualitative feedback from your collaborator and your audience about what they enjoyed most about the collaboration, and what they'd like to see more of in the future.

Remember, collaboration is an iterative process – the more you do it, the better you'll get at creating content and partnerships that truly resonate with your audience and drive meaningful results for your business.

Collaborating with influencers and other businesses on social media can be a game-changer for your brand – but it's not always easy. It takes time, effort, and a willingness to step outside your comfort zone and try something new.

But when you find the right collaborators, create amazing content together, and promote it effectively, the results can be truly incredible – from growing your following and engagement to driving sales and building long-term relationships and partnerships.

So what are you waiting for? Start brainstorming some collaboration ideas, reaching out to potential partners, and creating content that will wow your audience and take your social media presence to the next level!

And there you have it – a comprehensive guide to leveraging social media for business growth, from choosing the right platforms and creating a strategy to running ads and collaborating with influencers. I hope this has been helpful and inspiring as you navigate the ever-changing world of social media marketing. Remember, the key is to stay authentic, adaptable, and always put your audience first. Happy collaborating!

Chapter 7
Implementing Effective Email Marketing Strategies

Building Your Email List and Lead Magnets

Well hello there, email marketing master-in-the-making! Are you ready to take your online business to the next level with the power of email marketing? Because let me tell you, email is where the magic happens. It's where you get to build deep, personal relationships with your audience, deliver value straight to their inboxes, and ultimately, drive more sales and revenue for your business.

But here's the thing – none of that can happen if you don't have a solid email list to begin with. Your email list is your most valuable asset as an online business owner – it's a direct line of communication to your most engaged and loyal followers, and it's a list that you own and control, unlike your social media followers or search engine rankings.

So, how do you go about building an email list from scratch, or growing your existing list to epic proportions? Two words: lead magnets.

A lead magnet is basically a freebie or incentive that you offer to your website visitors in exchange for their email address. It's a way to provide upfront value and build trust with your audience, while also getting permission to keep in touch with them via email.

In this section, we'll dive into the nitty-gritty of creating irresistible lead magnets that your audience won't be able to resist, and building an email list that will be the foundation of your email marketing success. So grab a notepad (or a Google doc), and let's get started!

1. Understand the Importance of Email Marketing

Before we dive into the tactics of building your email list, let's take a moment to understand why email marketing is so crucial for your online business.

Email marketing allows you to:

- Build personal, one-on-one relationships with your subscribers and customers
- Deliver value, education, and entertainment straight to your audience's inboxes
- Promote your products, services, or offerings to a warm and engaged audience
- Automate your marketing and sales funnels to save time and increase conversions
- Segment your list based on interests, behaviors, or demographics to deliver more targeted and relevant content
- Analyze and optimize your email performance to continually improve your results and ROI
- In short, email marketing is one of the most effective and profitable ways to build and grow your online business – but it all starts with a high-quality email list.

2. Create an Irresistible Lead Magnet

Now that you understand the importance of email marketing, it's time to create a lead magnet that will attract your ideal subscribers like bees to honey.

A great lead magnet should be:
- Highly relevant and valuable to your target audience (solves a problem, answers a question, or satisfies a desire)
- Quick and easy to consume (think checklists, cheat sheets, templates, or short guides)
- Instantly accessible and deliverable (no waiting or hoops to jump through)
- Aligned with your overall brand and business goals (ties into your products, services, or mission)

Some examples of popular lead magnet formats include:
- Ebooks, guides, or whitepapers
- Checklists, cheat sheets, or resource lists
- Templates, swipe files, or blueprints
- Video trainings, webinars, or mini-courses
- Quizzes, assessments, or personalized reports
- When creating your lead magnet, be sure to:
- Choose a topic that your target audience is hungry for and actively searching for information on
- Create high-quality, valuable content that showcases your expertise and leaves your subscribers wanting more
- Design an eye-catching and professional cover or graphic that makes your lead magnet irresistible to download
- Write a compelling title and description that communicates the benefits and value of your lead magnet

3. Set Up Your Email Marketing Platform

Once you've created your lead magnet, it's time to set up your email marketing platform and opt-in forms to start collecting email addresses.

There are many email marketing platforms to choose from, such as:

- Mailchimp
- ConvertKit
- AWeber
- ActiveCampaign
- Constant Contact

When choosing an email marketing platform, consider factors like:
- Pricing and features (e.g. list size, automation, integrations)
- Ease of use and user interface
- Customer support and resources
- Deliverability and reputation
- Once you've chosen your platform, set up your account and create your first email list.
- Then, create an opt-in form or landing page where people can enter their email address to receive your lead magnet.

Be sure to:
- Place your opt-in form in a prominent location on your website (e.g. header, sidebar, footer, pop-up)
- Write compelling copy that communicates the benefits and value of signing up for your email list
- Include a clear and specific call-to-action (e.g. "Download your free guide now!")
- Test and optimize your opt-in forms to maximize conversions and sign-ups

4. Promote Your Lead Magnet

Now that you've created your lead magnet and set up your opt-in forms, it's time to start promoting it to your target audience!

There are many ways to promote your lead magnet, such as:
- Featuring it prominently on your website homepage and relevant blog posts or pages
- Sharing it on your social media profiles and in relevant groups or communities
- Running paid ads or promotions on social media, search engines, or other websites
- Partnering with other businesses or influencers in your niche to cross-promote each other's lead magnets
- Including a link to your lead magnet in your email signature, business cards, or other marketing materials

When promoting your lead magnet, be sure to:
- Tailor your messaging and targeting to your ideal audience and their specific pain points or desires
- Use eye-catching visuals and compelling copy to grab attention and communicate value
- Include a clear and specific call-to-action that encourages people to sign up for your email list
- Track your clicks, sign-ups, and conversions to continually optimize and improve your promotion strategies

5. Nurture Your Email List

Congratulations – you've built an email list of engaged and interested subscribers! But your work doesn't stop there. Now, it's time to nurture those relationships and keep your subscribers engaged and excited to hear from you.

To nurture your email list, be sure to:
- Send regular, valuable content that educates, entertains, or inspires your subscribers (aim for at least once a week)

- Segment your list based on interests, behaviors, or demographics to deliver more targeted and relevant content
- Personalize your emails with your subscribers' names, interests, or past behaviors to build stronger connections
- Encourage replies, feedback, and engagement from your subscribers to build two-way relationships
- Periodically clean and prune your list to remove inactive or bounced email addresses and maintain high deliverability and engagement rates

Remember, your email list is a long-term asset that requires consistent attention and care. But when you nurture it properly, it can become one of your most powerful and profitable tools for growing your online business.

Building an email list and creating irresistible lead magnets is not a one-time task – it's an ongoing process that requires creativity, experimentation, and iteration. But when you get it right, the payoff is immense – a loyal, engaged community of subscribers who trust you, value your expertise, and are eager to hear from you and buy from you again and again.

So what are you waiting for? Start brainstorming your next awesome lead magnet, setting up your email marketing platform, and promoting the heck out of it to your target audience. Your email list (and your business) will thank you!

Segmenting Your Subscribers and Personalizing Your Emails

Welcome back, email marketing rockstar! Now that you've built a healthy email list and started sending valuable content to your subscribers, it's time to take your email game to the next level with the power of segmentation and personalization.

Imagine this: instead of sending the same generic email blast to your entire list, you could send highly targeted, relevant, and personalized emails to specific segments of your audience based on their interests, behaviors, or characteristics. Sounds pretty awesome, right?

That's the magic of email segmentation and personalization – it allows you to create a more tailored and engaging email experience for your subscribers, which in turn leads to higher open rates, click-through rates, and conversions.

But how exactly do you segment your email list and personalize your emails? And what are some best practices and strategies to keep in mind?

Fear not – we've got you covered! In this section, we'll dive into the nitty-gritty of email segmentation and personalization, and give you all the tools and tactics you need to start sending emails that truly resonate with your unique audience.

So grab a cup of coffee (or tea, if that's more your style), and let's dive in!

1. Understand the Benefits of Segmentation and Personalization

Before we get into the how-to of segmentation and personalization, let's take a moment to understand why they're so powerful for your email marketing.

By segmenting your email list and personalizing your emails, you can:

- Deliver more relevant and valuable content to each subscriber based on their specific interests, needs, or behaviors
- Increase your email open rates, click-through rates, and overall engagement by making your emails feel more targeted and personal
- Build stronger relationships and trust with your subscribers by showing that you understand and care about their individual preferences and experiences
- Boost your email conversions and revenue by promoting the right products, services, or offers to the right people at the right time
- Stand out in a crowded inbox by creating a more memorable and personalized email experience that sets you apart from generic, one-size-fits-all email blasts
- In short, segmentation and personalization are the keys to unlocking the full potential of your email list and creating a more effective, profitable email marketing strategy.

2. Collect Relevant Subscriber Data

To effectively segment your email list and personalize your emails, you first need to collect relevant data about your subscribers.

There are many ways to collect subscriber data, such as:
- Asking for information in your email opt-in forms or sign-up process (e.g. name, location, interests, job title)
- Tracking subscriber behavior and engagement within your emails (e.g. opens, clicks, purchases)
- Integrating your email marketing platform with your website, e-commerce store, or other tools to collect data on subscriber actions and preferences
- Conducting surveys, quizzes, or polls to gather more detailed insights and feedback from your subscribers

When collecting subscriber data, be sure to:
- Only ask for information that is truly relevant and necessary for your segmentation and personalization goals (don't overwhelm subscribers with too many fields or questions)
- Be transparent about how you will use and protect subscriber data, and give subscribers the option to opt out or update their preferences at any time
- Regularly clean and update your subscriber data to ensure accuracy and relevance (e.g. removing bounced or inactive emails, updating changed information)
- The more relevant and up-to-date your subscriber data is, the more effectively you can segment your list and personalize your emails.

3. Create Meaningful Subscriber Segments

Once you've collected relevant subscriber data, it's time to start creating meaningful segments based on that data.

There are many ways to segment your email list, depending on your specific goals, audience, and business. Some common segmentation criteria include:

- Demographics (e.g. age, gender, location, job title)
- Interests or preferences (e.g. product categories, content topics, communication frequency)
- Behavior or engagement (e.g. email opens, clicks, purchases, website activity)
- Customer status (e.g. new subscribers, active customers, lapsed customers)
- Lead magnet or opt-in source (e.g. free guide, webinar, contest)

When creating your segments, consider:
- What specific groups or characteristics of subscribers would benefit from more targeted or personalized email content?
- What are the key differentiators or variables that influence subscriber needs, preferences, or behaviors?
- How can you use segmentation to better align your email content and offers with your business goals and subscriber expectations?
- Keep in mind that segments don't have to be mutually exclusive – a subscriber can belong to multiple segments based on different criteria (e.g. a 25-year-old female subscriber who clicked on a specific product link).
- The key is to create segments that are specific and actionable enough to inform your email content and strategy, without being so narrow that they limit your reach or relevance.

4. Tailor Your Email Content and Offers

Now that you've created your subscriber segments, it's time to start tailoring your email content and offers to each segment.

There are many ways to personalize your emails based on subscriber data and segments, such as:
- Using subscriber name or other personal details in the email subject line, greeting, or body copy
- Referencing subscriber location, interests, or past behavior to provide more relevant or localized content and recommendations
- Showcasing specific products, services, or offers that align with subscriber preferences or past purchases
- Adjusting email frequency, timing, or format based on subscriber engagement or preferences
- Including dynamic content blocks that change based on subscriber data or behavior (e.g. different product recommendations for different segments)

When personalizing your emails, aim to:
- Use subscriber data and insights to create a more relevant, valuable, and engaging email experience for each segment
- Balance personalization with privacy and respect for subscriber preferences (don't overuse or misuse personal data in a way that feels intrusive or creepy)
- Test and optimize your personalized email content and offers to continually improve performance and subscriber satisfaction

Keep in mind that personalization doesn't have to be complicated or time-consuming – even small touches like using a subscriber's name or referencing their past behavior can go a long way in making your emails feel more targeted and personal.

5. Analyze and Refine Your Segmentation and Personalization

- Like any aspect of email marketing, segmentation and personalization require ongoing analysis and refinement to ensure maximum effectiveness and ROI.
- Regularly review your email performance metrics (e.g. open rates, click-through rates, conversions) for each segment and personalized campaign to identify what's working well and what could be improved.
- Use A/B testing to experiment with different segmentation criteria, personalization tactics, or email content and offers, and see which variations drive the best results.
- Gather feedback and insights from your subscribers through surveys, reviews, or customer support interactions to better understand their preferences, needs, and experiences with your emails.
- Continuously update and refine your subscriber data and segments based on new information, behaviors, or feedback to ensure relevance and accuracy.

Remember, effective segmentation and personalization are not a one-time task, but an ongoing process of learning, experimentation, and optimization.

By leveraging the power of email segmentation and personalization, you can take your email marketing to the next level and create a more engaging, effective, and profitable email strategy that truly resonates with your unique audience.

It may take some time and effort to set up and optimize your segmentation and personalization tactics, but the payoff is well worth it – higher engagement, stronger relationships, and better business results.

So what are you waiting for? Start collecting relevant subscriber data, creating meaningful segments, and personalizing your emails like the email marketing rockstar you are!

Crafting Compelling Email Copy and Subject Lines

Alright, email marketing wordsmith! Now that you've mastered the art of segmentation and personalization, it's time to focus on the heart and soul of your emails – the copy and subject lines. Because let's face it, you could have the most targeted and personalized email in the world, but if your copy falls flat or your subject line fails to grab attention, your email is going straight to the trash folder.

But fear not – crafting compelling email copy and subject lines is a skill that anyone can learn with a little bit of creativity, psychology, and practice. And when you get it right, the impact on your email performance and business results can be massive.

Think about it – your subject line is the first thing your subscribers see when your email hits their inbox, and it's often the only thing that determines whether they open your email or not. And once they do open your email, your copy is what keeps them reading, clicking, and ultimately converting into customers or fans.

So, how do you write email copy and subject lines that stand out in a crowded inbox, pique curiosity, and inspire action? And what are some best practices and formulas to keep in mind?

Don't worry – we've got you covered! In this section, we'll dive into the art and science of email copywriting, and give you all the tips and techniques you need to start crafting emails that your subscribers can't resist opening and engaging with.

So grab your favorite pen (or keyboard), and let's get writing!

1. Understand the Goals and Elements of Email Copy

Before we dive into the specifics of email copywriting, let's take a moment to understand the goals and elements of effective email copy.

The primary goals of your email copy are to:

- Grab attention and generate interest in your email content and offers
- Communicate value and benefits to your subscribers, and show how your email is relevant and helpful to their needs or desires
- Build trust and relationships with your subscribers, and establish your brand voice and personality
- Inspire action and drive clicks, conversions, or other desired behaviors from your subscribers

To achieve these goals, your email copy should include the following key elements:

- A compelling subject line that entices subscribers to open your email
- A clear and attention-grabbing headline or opening line that hooks readers and sets the stage for your email content

- Concise and scannable body copy that communicates your main points and benefits in an easy-to-read format
- Relevant and engaging visuals (e.g. images, videos, GIFs) that support and enhance your copy
- A strong and specific call-to-action (CTA) that tells subscribers exactly what you want them to do next (e.g. "Shop now", "Download your free guide", "Register for the webinar")
- Keep these goals and elements in mind as you craft your email copy, and aim to create a cohesive and compelling message that resonates with your target audience.

2. Master the Art of Subject Lines

Now let's talk about the most important element of your email copy – the subject line.

Your subject line is like the headline of your email – it's what grabs your subscribers' attention and determines whether they open your email or not.

To write effective subject lines, aim to:

- Keep it short and sweet (ideally 50 characters or less) to ensure readability and avoid getting cut off in email previews
- Use actionable and benefit-driven language that communicates value and urgency (e.g. "Get 50% off your first order – today only!")
- Personalize the subject line with the subscriber's name, location, or other relevant data to increase relevance and open rates
- Avoid spammy or salesy words (e.g. "FREE", "Act now", "Guarantee") that can trigger spam filters or turn off subscribers

Test different subject line variations and styles (e.g. questions, lists, curiosity-based) to see what works best for your audience

Here are some examples of compelling subject lines:
- "10 secrets to a healthier, happier you "
- "[Name], your exclusive 24-hour discount is waiting! "
- "The one email hack that will change your life "
- "New [product] is here – be the first to try it!"

Remember, your subject line is the gatekeeper to your email – so make it count!

3. Write Clear and Compelling Body Copy

Once your subject line has done its job and gotten your email opened, it's time for your body copy to shine.

Your body copy should be clear, concise, and compelling, and should communicate the main points and benefits of your email in an easy-to-read format.

To write effective body copy, aim to:
- Start with a strong and attention-grabbing opening line that hooks readers and sets the stage for your email content
- Use short paragraphs, bullet points, and subheadings to break up your copy and make it scannable
- Highlight key points and benefits with bold or colored text, and use visuals to support and enhance your message
- Write in a conversational and relatable tone that reflects your brand voice and personality
- Focus on the reader and their needs or desires, and use "you" language to make your copy feel more personal and engaging

End with a clear and specific call-to-action that tells subscribers exactly what you want them to do next

Here's an example of compelling body copy:

"Hey [Name],

I hope this email finds you well! I wanted to quickly share with you a new product that I think you're going to love.

Introducing [Product Name] – the ultimate solution to [problem or desire]. With [key benefit 1], [key benefit 2], and [key benefit 3], [Product Name] is the perfect tool to help you [achieve desired outcome].

But don't just take my word for it – here's what some of our happy customers have to say:

"[Testimonial 1]" – [Customer Name]
"[Testimonial 2]" – [Customer Name]

Ready to try [Product Name] for yourself? Click the button below to get started – and as a special thank you for being a loyal subscriber, use code [Discount Code] at checkout for 20% off your first order!

[CTA Button: "Get [Product Name] Now!"]

Thanks for reading, and happy [benefit or outcome]!

[Your Name]"

See how the copy is clear, concise, and benefit-driven, and uses formatting and visuals to make the message more engaging and scannable? That's the power of effective body copy!

4. Test and Optimize Your Copy and Subject Lines

Like any element of email marketing, your copy and subject lines should be continually tested and optimized to ensure maximum effectiveness and ROI.

Use A/B testing to experiment with different subject line and copy variations, and see which ones drive the best open rates, click-through rates, and conversions.

Some elements to test include:
- Subject line length, style, and personalization
- Headline and opening line variations
- Body copy length, formatting, and tone
- Call-to-action text, placement, and design
- Images, videos, and other visuals
- Use your email marketing platform's analytics and reporting tools to track and analyze your test results, and identify the winning variations for each element.

Keep in mind that what works for one audience or email may not work for another – so it's important to continually test and optimize your copy and subject lines based on your unique subscribers and goals.

By mastering the art and science of email copywriting, you can create emails that not only get opened and read but also drive real results for your business – from increased engagement and conversions to stronger relationships and revenue.

It may take some time and practice to find your email copywriting groove, but the payoff is well worth it – a loyal and engaged subscriber base that can't wait to hear from you and buy from you.

So what are you waiting for? Start crafting subject lines that sizzle and copy that converts – and watch your email marketing soar to new heights!

Automating Your Email Campaigns and Sales Funnels

Hey there, email marketing automation aficionado! Are you ready to take your email game to the next level and start driving results on autopilot? Because let me tell you, email automation and sales funnels are where the real magic happens.

Imagine this: instead of manually sending out one-off emails to your subscribers and hoping for the best, you could create a series of automated email campaigns and sequences that nurture your leads, drive sales, and grow your business – all while you sleep, eat, or binge-watch your favorite show.

Sounds like a dream come true, right?

That's the power of email automation and sales funnels – they allow you to create personalized, targeted, and timely email experiences that guide your subscribers through their customer journey and ultimately convert them into loyal fans and customers.

But what exactly are email automation and sales funnels? And how do you create them in a way that feels authentic, valuable, and non-spammy?

Don't worry – we've got you covered! In this section, we'll dive into the nuts and bolts of email automation and sales funnels, and give you all the strategies and tools you need to start creating high-converting campaigns that work for your unique business and audience.

So grab a notepad (or a Google Doc), and let's dive in!

1. Understand the Basics of Email Automation

Before we get into the nitty-gritty of creating email automation campaigns and sales funnels, let's take a moment to understand what email automation is and how it works.

Email automation is the process of setting up pre-written email sequences that are automatically triggered based on specific subscriber actions, behaviors, or timelines.

Instead of manually sending out one-off emails to your subscribers, you can create a series of emails that are automatically sent out based on triggers like:

- Subscribing to your email list
- Abandoning a cart or not completing a purchase
- Clicking a specific link or engaging with a particular email
- Reaching a certain point in your sales funnel or customer journey
- Email automation allows you to create more personalized, relevant, and timely email experiences for your subscribers, while also saving you time and effort in the long run.
- Most email marketing platforms (like Mailchimp, ConvertKit, or ActiveCampaign) offer email automation features that allow you to easily create and manage your automated campaigns and sequences.

2. Map Out Your Customer Journey and Sales Funnel

- To create effective email automation campaigns and sales funnels, you first need to understand your customer journey and map out your sales funnel.

- Your customer journey is the path that your subscribers take from first discovering your brand to becoming loyal customers and advocates.
- Your sales funnel is the series of steps and stages that guide your subscribers through that journey and ultimately lead to a sale or conversion.
- A typical sales funnel might include stages like:
- **Awareness:** Subscribers first discover your brand through social media, ads, or other marketing channels.
- **Interest:** Subscribers engage with your content, visit your website, and sign up for your email list.
- **Consideration:** Subscribers learn more about your products or services, compare options, and evaluate their needs and budget.
- **Intent:** Subscribers show strong interest in buying, add items to their cart, or request more information.
- **Purchase:** Subscribers complete their purchase and become customers.
- **Loyalty:** Customers continue to engage with your brand, buy more products, and refer others.
- Map out your unique customer journey and sales funnel stages, and identify the key actions, triggers, and goals for each stage.
- This will help you create more targeted and relevant email automation campaigns and sequences that guide your subscribers through each stage and ultimately drive more conversions and revenue.

3. Create Email Automation Campaigns and Sequences

Now that you've mapped out your customer journey and sales funnel, it's time to start creating your email automation campaigns and sequences!

Here are some common types of email automation campaigns and sequences you can create:

- Welcome Series: A series of emails that welcome new subscribers to your email list, introduce your brand and values, and set expectations for future content and offers.
- Onboarding Sequence: A series of emails that guide new customers through the process of using your product or service, provide helpful resources and support, and encourage them to take key actions (like completing their profile or referring friends).
- Abandoned Cart Sequence: A series of emails that remind subscribers who added items to their cart but didn't complete their purchase, and offer incentives or urgency to encourage them to buy.
- Post-Purchase Sequence: A series of emails that thank customers for their purchase, provide helpful information and resources (like product tutorials or care instructions), and encourage them to leave a review or refer others.
- Re-Engagement Sequence: A series of emails that re-engage inactive subscribers who haven't opened or clicked your emails in a while, and offer incentives or personalized content to win them back.
- For each email automation campaign or sequence, aim to:
- Set clear goals and objectives for what you want to achieve (like increasing open rates, driving sales, or reducing churn)

- Segment your subscribers based on their unique characteristics, behaviors, or funnel stage
- Personalize your email content and offers based on each subscriber's interests, needs, and actions
- Use a clear and compelling subject line, body copy, and call-to-action (CTA) that aligns with your goals and resonates with your audience
- Test and optimize your email automation flows and content based on your results and feedback

4. Integrate Your Email Automation with Other Marketing Channels

To maximize the impact and ROI of your email automation campaigns and sales funnels, it's important to integrate them with your other marketing channels and tools.

Some ways to integrate your email automation include:
- Syncing your email list with your CRM or customer database to ensure accurate and up-to-date subscriber data
- Triggering email automation flows based on subscriber actions or behaviors on your website or app (like visiting a specific page, filling out a form, or completing a purchase)
- Retargeting your email subscribers with personalized ads or offers on social media or Google
- Incorporating email automation data and insights into your overall marketing analytics and reporting
- By integrating your email automation with your other marketing channels and tools, you can create a more seamless and cohesive customer experience that drives better results and ROI.

Segment your subscribers based on their unique characteristics, behaviors, or funnel stage
- Personalize your email content and offers based on each subscriber's interests, needs, and actions
- Use a clear and compellinsubject line, body copy, and call-to-action (CTA) that aligns with your goals and resonates with your audience
- Test and optimize your email automation flows and content based on your results and feedback

4. Integrate Your Email Automation with Other Marketing Channels

To maximize the impact and ROI of your email automation campaigns and sales funnels, it's important to integrate them with your other marketing channels and tools.

Some ways to integrate your email automation include:
- Syncing your email list with your CRM or customer database to ensure accurate and up-to-date subscriber data
- Triggering email automation flows based on subscriber actions or behaviors on your website or app (like visiting a specific page, filling out a form, or completing a purchase)
- Retargeting your email subscribers with personalized ads or offers on social media or Google
- Incorporating email automation data and insights into your overall marketing analytics and reporting
- By integrating your email automation with your other marketing channels and tools, you can create a more seamless and cohesive customer experience that drives better results and ROI.

5. Measure and Optimize Your Email Automation Performance

Like any aspect of email marketing, your email automation campaigns and sales funnels require ongoing measurement and optimization to ensure maximum performance and ROI.

Use your email marketing platform's analytics and reporting tools to track key metrics like:

- Open rates, click-through rates, and conversion rates for each email and automation flow
- Subscriber engagement, retention, and churn rates over time
- Revenue and average order value (AOV) generated from each automation campaign or sequence
- Use these insights to identify what's working well and what could be improved, and continually test and optimize your email automation content, timing, and targeting.

Some elements to test and optimize include:

- Subject line and preview text variations
- Email layout, design, and copy
- Personalization and segmentation criteria
- Timing and frequency of emails
- Landing pages and conversion flows

By continually measuring and optimizing your email automation performance, you can create more effective and profitable campaigns that drive long-term business growth and success.

Email automation and sales funnels are powerful tools that can transform your email marketing from a one-off tactic to a holistic, customer-centric strategy that drives real results and revenue for your business.

By mapping out your customer journey, creating targeted and personalized automation campaigns, integrating with your other marketing channels, and continually optimizing your performance, you can create email experiences that not only engage and convert your subscribers but also build long-term relationships and loyalty.

It may take some trial and error to find the right email automation approach for your unique business and audience, but the payoff is well worth it – a steady stream of leads, sales, and growth that runs on autopilot while you focus on what you do best.

So what are you waiting for? Start mapping out your customer journey, creating your first email automation campaign, and watching your business soar to new heights!

Chapter 8
Scaling Your Online Business and Increasing Revenue

Diversifying Your Income Streams and Offerings

Congratulations, online business owner extraordinaire! You've built a solid foundation for your online business, with a targeted niche, compelling offers, and a growing audience of loyal fans and customers. But now, it's time to take things to the next level and start scaling your business for even greater impact, freedom, and revenue.

And one of the most powerful ways to do that is by diversifying your income streams and offerings.

Think about it – when you first started your online business, you probably focused on creating one core product or service that served your target audience and aligned with your skills and passions. And that's a great place to start! But as your business grows and evolves, relying on just one income stream can actually limit your potential and put your business at risk.

By diversifying your income streams and offerings, you can:
- Reach new audiences and markets that may not have been interested in your original product or service
- Provide more value and solutions to your existing audience, and increase their lifetime customer value
- Protect your business from market shifts, algorithm changes, or other external factors that could impact your main income stream

- Increase your revenue potential and profit margins by creating multiple, complementary income streams that work together
- Give yourself more creative freedom and flexibility to experiment with new ideas, formats, and platforms

Sounds pretty great, right?

But with so many potential income streams and offerings to choose from – from digital products and courses to coaching and affiliate marketing – it can be overwhelming to know where to start.

Fear not – we've got you covered! In this section, we'll explore some of the most effective and popular ways to diversify your income streams and offerings, and give you a step-by-step plan for adding them to your online business.

So grab a pen and paper (or a fresh Google Doc), and let's dive in!

1. Assess Your Current Income Streams and Offerings
Before you start adding new income streams and offerings to your business, it's important to take stock of what you already have and how it's performing.
Make a list of your current products, services, and income streams, and ask yourself:
- What's working well and generating the most revenue and impact?
- What's not working as well or feels misaligned with your goals and values?

- What do your customers and audience love most about your offerings, and what do they wish you offered more of?
- What are your profit margins and scalability potential for each income stream?
- Use this analysis to identify your strengths, weaknesses, opportunities, and threats (SWOT) as a business, and to prioritize which income streams and offerings to focus on expanding or optimizing first.

2. Identify Your Audience's Needs and Desires

To create new income streams and offerings that truly resonate with your audience and drive sales, you need to deeply understand their needs, desires, and pain points.

Conduct market research and gather feedback from your existing customers and audience through surveys, interviews, and analytics data.

Look for patterns and insights around:

- What challenges or goals your audience is struggling with most
- What solutions or resources they're currently using or searching for
- What formats or platforms they prefer for consuming content and making purchases
- What price points and payment options they're most comfortable with
- Use these insights to brainstorm new product, service, or content ideas that address your audience's most pressing needs and desires, and that align with your unique skills, passions, and brand.

3. Brainstorm and Prioritize New Income Stream Ideas

Now that you have a better understanding of your current business performance and audience needs, it's time to start generating ideas for new income streams and offerings!

Some popular income stream ideas for online businesses include:
- Digital products (ebooks, courses, templates, printables, etc.)
- Coaching or consulting services
- Membership sites or subscriptions
- Affiliate marketing or sponsorships
- Physical products (merchandise, print-on-demand, etc.)
- Freelance services (writing, design, development, etc.)
- Speaking or workshop engagements
- Advertising or sponsored content

Brainstorm a big list of potential income stream ideas that align with your skills, passions, and audience needs, and then prioritize them based on factors like:
- Revenue potential and profit margins
- Setup and ongoing time/resource investment
- Audience demand and competition
- Alignment with your brand and values
- Scalability and automation potential
- Choose the top 1-3 income stream ideas that feel most exciting and feasible for you to implement in the next 90 days, and create a plan for bringing them to life.

4. Develop and Launch Your New Offerings

With your new income stream ideas prioritized and planned out, it's time to start developing and launching them!

For each new offering, create a detailed project plan that outlines:

- Your target audience and unique value proposition
- Your content or product creation process and timeline
- Your pricing and payment options
- Your marketing and sales strategies
- Your delivery and fulfillment systems
- Your customer support and retention plans

Break your project plan down into smaller, actionable tasks and milestones, and assign them to yourself or your team members with clear deadlines and expectations.

As you develop your new offerings, be sure to:
- Validate your ideas with your target audience through surveys, beta tests, or pre-sales
- Create high-quality, valuable content or products that reflect your brand and expertise
- Set up efficient, scalable systems and processes for delivery, payment, and support
- Incorporate customer feedback and insights into your iterations and improvements

When you're ready to launch, create a compelling marketing and sales campaign that includes:
- Email marketing and automated sequences
- Social media and content marketing
- Paid advertising and partnerships
- Affiliate and referral programs
- Launch bonuses and limited-time offers

Remember, launching a new income stream or offering is just the beginning – be prepared to continually market, optimize, and improve it based on your results and customer feedback.

5. Evaluate and Optimize Your Income Stream Portfolio

As you add new income streams and offerings to your business, it's important to regularly evaluate and optimize your overall income stream portfolio for maximum revenue, impact, and sustainability.

At least once a quarter, review your income and expense reports, customer feedback and analytics, and team capacity and performance for each income stream.

Look for patterns and insights around:

- Which income streams are generating the most revenue and profit, and which are underperforming or draining resources?
- Which offerings are resonating most with your audience and driving the best results and feedback?
- Which systems or processes are working efficiently and effectively, and which need improvement or automation?
- Which team members or partners are contributing most to the success and growth of each income stream, and which may need additional support or training?

Based on your analysis, make data-driven decisions to:

- Double down on your most profitable and impactful income streams, and allocate more resources and focus to growing and optimizing them
- Streamline or sunset underperforming or misaligned income streams, and redirect those resources to more promising opportunities
- Continuously improve and automate your systems and processes to increase efficiency, scalability, and profitability
- Invest in your team and partners' growth and development to support the long-term success and sustainability of your income stream portfolio

Remember, diversifying your income streams and offerings is an ongoing, iterative process – not a one-time event. By continually evaluating and optimizing your portfolio, you can create a resilient, profitable, and impactful online business that stands the test of time.

Diversifying your income streams and offerings is one of the most powerful ways to scale your online business and increase your revenue, impact, and freedom. By providing more value and solutions to your audience, reaching new markets and customers, and creating multiple, complementary revenue sources, you can build a thriving, sustainable business that supports your dreams and lifestyle.

But it's not always easy – it requires strategic planning, creative thinking, and consistent execution to successfully add and manage multiple income streams. There will be challenges and learning curves along the way, but with persistence, adaptability, and a focus on serving your audience, you can overcome them and emerge stronger and more profitable than ever.

So dream big, start small, and take action today to diversify your income streams and offerings – your future self (and bank account) will thank you!

Outsourcing and Building a Team

Alright, online business rockstar – let's talk about one of the most important secrets to scaling your business and increasing your revenue: outsourcing and building a team.

Here's the thing – as a solopreneur or small business owner, you might be used to wearing all the hats and doing everything yourself. And in the early stages of your business, that can be a great way to keep costs low and maintain control over your vision and brand.

But as your business grows and evolves, trying to do everything yourself can actually hold you back from reaching your full potential. There are only so many hours in the day, and only so many skills and tasks that you can master on your own. At some point, you'll hit a ceiling where you simply can't take on any more work or responsibilities without sacrificing your quality, sanity, or personal life.

That's where outsourcing and building a team comes in – by leveraging other people's time, skills, and expertise, you can:

- Free up your time and energy to focus on your zone of genius and the high-level tasks that only you can do
- Expand your capacity and output without working longer or harder hours
- Bring in fresh perspectives, ideas, and skills that complement and enhance your own
- Provide better, faster, and more comprehensive service and support to your customers and clients
- Create a more scalable, sustainable, and valuable business that can grow beyond yourself

Sounds amazing, right?

But if you're used to being a one-person show, the idea of outsourcing and building a team can feel overwhelming, scary, or even impossible. Where do you start? How do you find the right people? And how do you ensure that your team is aligned with your vision, values, and standards?

Don't worry – we've got you covered! In this section, we'll walk you through the step-by-step process of outsourcing and building a team for your online business, and give you the tools and strategies you need to make it a success.

So grab your favorite beverage (coffee, tea, or maybe even a celebratory glass of champagne), and let's get started!

1. Identify Your Needs and Priorities
Before you start outsourcing or hiring, you need to get clear on what tasks, skills, and roles you actually need help with.
Make a list of all the tasks and responsibilities that you currently handle in your business, and then categorize them into three buckets:
- Tasks that only you can do, based on your unique skills, knowledge, or vision (e.g. high-level strategy, content creation, client relationships)
- Tasks that you enjoy doing and are good at, but that could be delegated or automated to free up your time and energy (e.g. social media, email marketing, customer support)
- Tasks that you don't enjoy, aren't good at, or that are outside of your zone of genius (e.g. bookkeeping, web development, graphic design)

For each task or role in the second and third buckets, ask yourself:
- How much time and energy does this task currently take up, and what could you do with that time and energy if it were freed up?
- What skills, experience, or qualifications would someone need to excel at this task or role?
- What level of quality, speed, and communication do you expect from someone handling this task or role?
- What is your budget and ideal payment structure for outsourcing or hiring for this task or role?
- Use your answers to these questions to create a clear, detailed job description or project brief for each task or role you want to outsource or hire for.

2. Find and Vet Potential Team Members

With your needs and priorities identified, it's time to start finding and vetting potential team members to help you bring your vision to life!

There are a few main ways to find great team members:
- Referrals from your network: Ask your business friends, colleagues, or mentors if they know anyone who might be a good fit for your needs.
- Online job boards or marketplaces: Post your job description or project on sites like LinkedIn, Indeed, Upwork, or Fiverr to reach a wide pool of candidates.
- Social media: Share your job or project on your social media channels, and ask your followers to spread the word or recommend anyone they know.

Agencies or service providers: Look for specialized agencies or service providers that offer the skills or services you need, like virtual assistants, bookkeepers, or web developers.

For each task or role in the second and third buckets, ask yourself:
- How much time and energy does this task currently take up, and what could you do with that time and energy if it were freed up?
- What skills, experience, or qualifications would someone need to excel at this task or role?
- What level of quality, speed, and communication do you expect from someone handling this task or role?
- What is your budget and ideal payment structure for outsourcing or hiring for this task or role?
- Use your answers to these questions to create a clear, detailed job description or project brief for each task or role you want to outsource or hire for.

2. Find and Vet Potential Team Members

With your needs and priorities identified, it's time to start finding and vetting potential team members to help you bring your vision to life!

There are a few main ways to find great team members:
- Referrals from your network: Ask your business friends, colleagues, or mentors if they know anyone who might be a good fit for your needs.
- Online job boards or marketplaces: Post your job description or project on sites like LinkedIn, Indeed, Upwork, or Fiverr to reach a wide pool of candidates.
- Social media: Share your job or project on your social media channels, and ask your followers to spread the word or recommend anyone they know.

Agencies or service providers: Look for specialized agencies or service providers that offer the skills or services you need, like virtual assistants, bookkeepers, or web developers.

Once you have a pool of potential candidates, vet them carefully to ensure they're a good fit for your business and needs:
- Review their resume, portfolio, or work samples to assess their skills, experience, and quality of work
- Schedule an interview or trial project to get a sense of their communication style, work ethic, and alignment with your values and vision
- Ask for references or testimonials from past clients or employers to verify their track record and reliability
- Clearly communicate your expectations, timeline, and budget upfront to ensure everyone is on the same page
- Don't rush the hiring process – take your time to find the right person or team who can help you achieve your goals and grow your business.

3. Onboard and Train Your Team

Congratulations – you've found some amazing team members to help you take your business to the next level! Now, it's time to set them up for success with a thorough onboarding and training process.

Your onboarding process should include:
- A clear, written agreement or contract that outlines the scope of work, deliverables, timeline, payment terms, and any other important details
- Access to any necessary tools, systems, or resources they'll need to do their job (e.g. project management software, brand guidelines, content templates)
- An orientation or kickoff meeting to introduce them to your business, your team, and your goals and expectations

A training or learning plan to help them develop the skills and knowledge they need to excel in their role

As you train your team, be sure to:
- Provide clear, detailed instructions and examples for each task or project
- Give regular feedback and guidance to help them improve and grow in their role
- Encourage questions, ideas, and collaboration to foster a positive, productive team culture
- Celebrate wins and milestones along the way to keep everyone motivated and engaged

Remember, investing time and energy into onboarding and training your team upfront will pay off in the long run with better quality work, higher retention, and a more cohesive, aligned team.

4. Communicate and Collaborate Effectively

Effective communication and collaboration are key to building a high-performing, engaged team – especially if you're working with remote or freelance team members.

Set up clear communication channels and expectations from the start:
- Choose a primary communication tool (e.g. email, Slack, Zoom) and establish guidelines for response times, availability, and etiquette
- Schedule regular check-ins or team meetings to align on goals, progress, and any issues or opportunities
- Create a shared project management system (e.g. Asana, Trello, ClickUp) to track tasks, deadlines, and deliverables and keep everyone on the same page
- Encourage open, honest, and respectful communication and feedback among team members

Foster collaboration and teamwork by:
- Clearly defining roles, responsibilities, and expectations for each team member
- Encouraging cross-functional collaboration and idea-sharing among team members with different skills and perspectives
- Providing opportunities for team bonding and relationship-building, like virtual happy hours or team-building activities
- Leading by example with a positive, supportive, and inclusive team culture

Remember, communication and collaboration are ongoing processes – be proactive in addressing any issues or conflicts that arise, and continually look for ways to improve and optimize your team's workflows and dynamics.

5. Evaluate and Optimize Your Team

As your business and team grow and evolve, it's important to regularly evaluate and optimize your team structure, performance, and culture.

At least quarterly, assess your team's:
- Productivity and performance: Are they meeting or exceeding their goals and deliverables? Are there any bottlenecks or inefficiencies that need to be addressed?
- Skills and capacity: Do you have the right mix of skills and experience on your team to support your current and future business needs? Are there any gaps or redundancies that need to be filled or streamlined?
- Engagement and satisfaction: Are your team members happy, motivated, and fulfilled in their roles? Do they feel supported, appreciated, and aligned with your business values and vision?

Cost and ROI: Are you getting a positive return on your investment in your team? Are there any areas where you could optimize costs or increase revenue and profitability? Based on your evaluation, make data-driven decisions to:
- Provide additional training, resources, or support to help team members improve their skills and performance
- Adjust roles, responsibilities, or team structure to better align with your business needs and goals
- Implement new processes, tools, or systems to increase efficiency, collaboration, and productivity
- Recognize and reward high-performing team members with bonuses, promotions, or other incentives
- Address any issues or conflicts proactively and respectfully, and make changes or tough decisions as needed to maintain a positive, productive team culture

Remember, building and managing a team is an ongoing, iterative process – be open to feedback, willing to adapt and experiment, and committed to creating a team and culture that brings out the best in everyone.

Outsourcing and building a team can be one of the most transformative and rewarding things you do for your online business – but it's not always easy. It requires a significant investment of time, energy, and resources to find the right people, train and manage them effectively, and create a team culture that aligns with your values and vision.

But when you get it right, the payoff is immeasurable – a business that can scale and thrive beyond your individual efforts, a team of talented, dedicated people who share your passion and purpose, and a greater impact and legacy than you ever could have achieved alone.

So start small, but think big – identify one key task or role that you can outsource or hire for today, and take the first step towards building the team and business of your dreams. Your future self (and your customers, your family, and the world) will thank you!

Analyzing Your Metrics and Making Data-Driven Decisions

Well, hello there, my data-driven dynamo! Are you ready to take your online business to the next level with the power of metrics and analytics? Because let me tell you, in today's digital landscape, data is the new currency – and if you're not using it to inform and optimize your business decisions, you're leaving money (and growth) on the table.

But I get it – with so many different metrics and data points to track and analyze, it can feel overwhelming and confusing to know where to start or what to focus on. Should you be looking at your website traffic, your social media engagement, your email open rates, your conversion rates, or all of the above? And how do you turn all those numbers into actionable insights and strategies that actually move the needle for your business?

Fear not, my friend – that's exactly what we're going to cover in this section! We'll break down the key metrics and analytics you need to be tracking for your online business, and give you a step-by-step framework for using that data to make informed, strategic decisions that drive real results.

So grab your favorite data visualization tool (or a trusty spreadsheet), and let's dive in!

1. Identify Your Key Performance Indicators (KPIs)
The first step in making data-driven decisions for your online business is to identify your key performance indicators (KPIs) – the metrics that are most critical to your business goals and success.

Your KPIs will depend on your specific business model, niche, and stage of growth, but some common ones include:
- Website traffic and engagement: Unique visitors, pageviews, bounce rate, time on site, etc.
- Email marketing: Subscribers, open rates, click-through rates, conversion rates, etc.
- Social media: Followers, likes, comments, shares, click-throughs, etc.
- Sales and revenue: Transactions, average order value, customer lifetime value, profit margins, etc.
- Customer acquisition and retention: New customers, repeat customers, churn rate, etc.

To identify your KPIs, ask yourself:
- What are my top business goals and objectives? (e.g. increase brand awareness, drive more leads and sales, improve customer loyalty)
- What metrics will help me measure progress towards those goals? (e.g. website traffic, email subscribers, revenue)
- What benchmarks or targets do I want to hit for each metric? (e.g. 10,000 monthly website visitors, $10,000 monthly revenue)
- What data do I need to track and analyze to calculate those metrics? (e.g. Google Analytics, email marketing platform, e-commerce platform)
- Once you've identified your KPIs, make sure you have the right tools and systems in place to track and measure them consistently and accurately.

2. Set Up Your Data Tracking and Reporting

With your KPIs identified, it's time to set up your data tracking and reporting systems to make sure you're collecting the right data and turning it into actionable insights.

There are a variety of tools and platforms you can use to track and analyze your online business metrics, depending on your needs and budget:

- Google Analytics: A free website analytics tool that tracks your website traffic, user behavior, and conversions.
- Email marketing platforms: Tools like Mailchimp, ConvertKit, or ActiveCampaign that track your email subscribers, open rates, click-through rates, and more.
- Social media analytics: Native analytics tools within each social media platform (e.g. Facebook Insights, Twitter Analytics) or third-party tools like Hootsuite or Sprout Social.
- E-commerce platforms: Tools like Shopify, WooCommerce, or Stripe that track your sales, revenue, and customer data.
- Business intelligence and data visualization tools: More advanced tools like Tableau, Looker, or Google Data Studio that help you combine and visualize data from multiple sources.

When setting up your data tracking and reporting, be sure to:

- Install the necessary tracking codes or pixels on your website and other online properties
- Integrate your different data sources and platforms to get a holistic view of your customer journey and funnel

- Create dashboards or reports that showcase your KPIs and other important metrics in a clear, visual way
- Set up alerts or notifications for any significant changes or anomalies in your data
- Remember, the goal is not just to collect data, but to turn it into insights and actions that help you optimize and grow your business.

3. Analyze Your Data and Identify Trends and Insights

Once you have your data tracking and reporting set up, it's time to start analyzing your data to identify trends, patterns, and insights that can inform your business decisions.

Regularly review your dashboards and reports (at least weekly or monthly) to look for:

- Overall trends: Are your key metrics increasing, decreasing, or staying flat over time? What might be causing those changes?
- Segmented insights: How do your metrics vary by different segments or dimensions, like traffic source, device type, customer demographics, product category, etc.? Are there any significant differences or opportunities within those segments?
- Correlations and relationships: Are there any metrics that seem to be correlated or have a cause-and-effect relationship? For example, do your email open rates tend to increase when you send more personalized subject lines, or do your sales tend to spike when you run certain promotions?

Anomalies and outliers: Are there any data points that seem unusually high or low compared to your normal range or expectations? What might be causing those anomalies, and do they warrant further investigation or action?

As you analyze your data, try to:
- Ask questions and form hypotheses about what the data is telling you and why
- Look for both positive and negative insights – areas where you're doing well and areas where you could improve
- Compare your data to industry benchmarks or your own historical performance to get a sense of how you stack up and where you have room to grow
- Use data visualization techniques (like charts, graphs, and heatmaps) to make the insights more clear and compelling

4. Turn Your Insights into Actions and Experiments

Data and insights are only valuable if you use them to take action and drive results for your business. So once you've analyzed your data and identified key insights, it's time to turn those insights into specific, measurable actions and experiments.

For each insight or opportunity you identify, brainstorm potential actions or changes you could make to your business strategy, tactics, or operations, such as:
- Optimizing your website or landing pages to improve user experience and conversions
- Adjusting your email marketing copy, timing, or segmentation to increase opens and clicks
- Tweaking your social media content, ads, or targeting to drive more engagement and traffic
- Adding new products, features, or promotions to your offerings based on customer behavior and preferences
- Investing more resources or budget into your top-performing marketing channels or campaigns

- Once you have a list of potential actions, prioritize them based on their potential impact, feasibility, and alignment with your overall business goals and resources.
- Then, for each high-priority action, create a specific, measurable experiment or test to validate its impact and ROI, such as:
- A/B testing different versions of a website or email to see which one performs better
- Piloting a new product or feature with a small group of customers before rolling it out more broadly
- Running a limited-time promotion or discount to see how it affects sales and customer acquisition
- Reallocating budget or resources from an underperforming channel to a higher-performing one and measuring the results

As you run your experiments and tests, be sure to:
- Set clear, measurable goals and hypotheses for each experiment (e.g. "If we change the headline on our landing page to X, we expect to see a 10% increase in conversions")
- Track and measure the relevant metrics and data points for each experiment
- Compare the results of your experiments to your original hypotheses and goals to determine their success and learnings
- Document and share your experiment results and insights with your team and stakeholders to facilitate learning and iteration

5. Continuously Learn, Iterate, and Optimize

- Making data-driven decisions for your online business is not a one-time event, but an ongoing process of learning, experimentation, and optimization.
- As you implement changes and experiments based on your data insights, continue to track and measure their impact and results over time.
- Use those results to refine your hypotheses, identify new opportunities or challenges, and iterate on your strategies and tactics accordingly.
- Continuously seek out new data sources, tools, and best practices to stay on the cutting edge of your industry and customer needs.
- Foster a culture of data-driven decision making and experimentation within your team and organization, and empower everyone to use data to inform and improve their work.
- Celebrate your successes and learnings along the way, and use them to build momentum and confidence in your ability to use data to drive growth and innovation.

Remember, the most successful online businesses are the ones that are constantly learning, adapting, and evolving based on data and customer feedback – so embrace the journey and enjoy the ride!

Analyzing your metrics and making data-driven decisions can be one of the most powerful and transformative things you do for your online business – but it's not always easy. It requires a significant investment of time, resources, and skills to set up the right tracking and reporting systems, analyze and interpret the data effectively, and turn those insights into meaningful actions and results.

But when you commit to a data-driven approach to your business, the rewards can be game-changing – from increased traffic, leads, and sales to improved customer satisfaction, retention, and loyalty. By letting the data guide your decisions and strategies, you can take the guesswork and risk out of growing your business, and create a sustainable, scalable model for long-term success.

So start small, but think big – identify one key metric or question you want to explore with data, and take the first step towards building a data-driven culture and mindset in your business. Your future self (and your bottom line) will thank you!

And there you have it – a comprehensive guide to scaling your online business and increasing your revenue, from diversifying your income streams and building a team to making data-driven decisions and optimizing your growth. I hope this has been helpful and inspiring as you take your business to the next level and achieve your wildest dreams. Remember, success is not a destination, but a journey – so enjoy the ride and never stop learning and growing!

Continuously Improving Your Products and Services

Hey there, you product perfecting prodigy! Are you ready to take your online business to the next level by continuously improving your products and services? Because let me tell you, in today's fast-paced and competitive digital landscape, the businesses that thrive are the ones that never stop innovating, iterating, and elevating their offerings to better serve their customers and stay ahead of the curve.

But I know what you might be thinking – "I already have a great product or service that my customers love! Why should I keep changing or improving it?" Well, my friend, there are a few key reasons why continuous improvement is not just important, but essential for the long-term success and growth of your business:

1. **Customer needs and expectations are always evolving.**
   - What your customers want and need from your products or services today may not be the same as what they want and need tomorrow, next month, or next year.
   - As new technologies, trends, and competitors emerge in your industry, your customers' preferences and behaviors will likely shift and change as well.
   - By continuously gathering feedback, analyzing data, and anticipating your customers' evolving needs, you can stay ahead of the curve and provide them with the most relevant, valuable, and delightful experiences possible.

2. Continuous improvement drives innovation and differentiation.

In a crowded and noisy online marketplace, it's not enough to just have a good product or service – you need to have a truly great and unique one that stands out from the competition.

By continuously improving and iterating on your offerings, you can unlock new opportunities for innovation, creativity, and differentiation that set you apart and make you the go-to choice for your target customers.

Whether it's adding new features, enhancing the user experience, or creating entirely new products or services that complement your existing ones, continuous improvement helps you stay fresh, relevant, and exciting in the eyes of your customers.

3. Continuous improvement enhances efficiency and profitability.

Improving your products and services isn't just about adding bells and whistles – it's also about streamlining your processes, reducing waste and costs, and increasing your overall efficiency and profitability.

By continuously analyzing your operations, identifying areas for improvement, and implementing lean and agile methodologies, you can optimize your resources, time, and budget to deliver better results with less effort and expense.

This not only helps you boost your bottom line, but also frees up more capacity and bandwidth to focus on higher-value activities and initiatives that drive your business forward.

4. Continuous improvement builds customer loyalty and advocacy.
When you consistently demonstrate a commitment to improving your products and services based on your customers' needs and feedback, you build deeper trust, loyalty, and advocacy with your audience.

By showing that you value their input, care about their success, and are always striving to do better for them, you create a strong emotional connection and relationship that goes beyond just a transactional exchange.

This can lead to higher customer retention, repeat business, and positive word-of-mouth referrals that help you acquire new customers and grow your brand reputation and reach.

So, now that you understand the why behind continuously improving your products and services, let's dive into the how – the specific strategies, frameworks, and best practices you can use to make continuous improvement a core part of your business DNA.

1. Gather and Analyze Customer Feedback and Data
The first and most critical step in continuously improving your products and services is to gather and analyze a steady stream of customer feedback and data – both qualitative and quantitative.

Some key ways to collect customer feedback include:
- Surveys and questionnaires (e.g. NPS, CSAT, product-market fit)
- Customer interviews and focus groups
- User testing and beta programs
- Social media and online reviews

- Support tickets and live chat transcripts

By regularly soliciting and synthesizing customer feedback across multiple channels and touchpoints, you can gain deep insights into what's working well, what's not, and what opportunities exist for improvement and innovation.

- In addition to direct customer feedback, you should also be tracking and analyzing key metrics and data points related to your products and services, such as:
- Usage and engagement metrics (e.g. adoption rate, active users, feature usage)
- Financial metrics (e.g. revenue, margin, customer lifetime value)
- Operational metrics (e.g. support volume, resolution time, defect rate)
- Competitive metrics (e.g. market share, win/loss rate)
- By combining qualitative feedback with quantitative data, you can get a holistic and objective view of your products and services' performance, and identify high-impact areas for improvement.

2. Prioritize and Implement Improvements and Iterations

Once you've gathered and analyzed your customer feedback and data, the next step is to prioritize and implement specific improvements and iterations to your products and services.

To prioritize your improvements, consider factors such as:
- Impact: How much value will this improvement deliver to your customers and your business?
- Effort: How much time, resources, and complexity will be required to implement this improvement?
- Urgency: How critical or time-sensitive is this improvement based on customer needs or market trends?

- Alignment: How well does this improvement align with your overall business goals, strategy, and brand?
- Based on these factors, you can create a prioritized roadmap or backlog of improvements, and assign them to specific teams or individuals for implementation.

As you implement your improvements, be sure to:
- Break them down into smaller, manageable tasks and milestones
- Set clear goals, requirements, and success criteria for each improvement
- Allocate the necessary resources, budget, and timeline for each improvement
- Communicate and coordinate with all relevant stakeholders and teams
- Test and validate your improvements with customers before fully launching them

Remember, the goal is not to make drastic or disruptive changes all at once, but rather to make continuous, incremental improvements that add up to significant value and impact over time.

3. Foster a Culture of Experimentation and Learning

To truly embrace continuous improvement as a core part of your business DNA, you need to foster a culture of experimentation and learning across your entire organization.

This means encouraging and empowering your teams to:
- Constantly question the status quo and challenge assumptions
- Generate and test new ideas and hypotheses for improving your products and services

- Embrace failure as an opportunity for learning and growth, rather than a sign of weakness or incompetence
- Share and celebrate successes, learnings, and best practices across teams and department
- Invest in ongoing training, development, and learning opportunities to stay up-to-date with the latest trends and skills

To support this culture of experimentation and learning, you should:

- Set clear expectations and goals around innovation and continuous improvement
- Provide the necessary tools, resources, and support for experimentation and learning
- Recognize and reward individuals and teams who demonstrate a commitment to continuous improvement and learning
- Lead by example and model the behaviors and mindset of continuous improvement yourself

By creating a safe and supportive environment for experimentation and learning, you can unleash the full potential and creativity of your teams, and drive meaningful and sustainable improvements to your products and services over time.

4. Collaborate with Partners and Stakeholders

Continuous improvement isn't just an internal process – it also involves collaborating with external partners and stakeholders who can provide valuable insights, resources, and support for improving your products and services.

Some key partners and stakeholders to collaborate with include:

- Customers and users: Engage them in co-creation and feedback sessions to gather input and ideas for improvements.
- Suppliers and vendors: Work with them to optimize your supply chain, reduce costs, and improve quality and reliability.
- Industry experts and thought leaders: Learn from their best practices, insights, and innovations to stay ahead of the curve.
- Competitors and peers: Benchmark your products and services against theirs, and identify opportunities for differentiation and improvement.
- Investors and advisors: Leverage their expertise, networks, and resources to support your continuous improvement efforts.

By building strong relationships and partnerships with these stakeholders, you can tap into a wealth of knowledge, perspectives, and capabilities that can help you accelerate and amplify your continuous improvement initiatives.

5. Measure and Communicate Your Results and Impact

Finally, to ensure that your continuous improvement efforts are delivering real and meaningful results and impact, you need to measure and communicate your progress and outcomes regularly.

Some key metrics and indicators to track and report on include:

- Customer satisfaction and loyalty (e.g. NPS, CSAT, retention rate)
- Revenue and profitability (e.g. sales growth, margin improvement)

- Operational efficiency and quality (e.g. cycle time, defect rate)
- Employee engagement and productivity (e.g. satisfaction score, output per employee)
- Innovation and differentiation (e.g. new products launched, patents filed)
- By setting clear goals and targets for these metrics, and regularly measuring and reporting on your progress against them, you can demonstrate the tangible value and ROI of your continuous improvement efforts.
- In addition to internal reporting, you should also communicate your continuous improvement results and impact to external stakeholders, such as:
- Customers: Share how your improvements are benefiting them and enhancing their experience.
- Partners: Highlight how your improvements are strengthening your relationships and creating new opportunities for collaboration.
- Investors: Demonstrate how your improvements are driving growth, profitability, and competitive advantage for your business.
- Media and influencers: Showcase your improvements as examples of innovation and thought leadership in your industry.

By proactively and transparently communicating your continuous improvement results and impact, you can build trust, credibility, and advocacy with your stakeholders, and create a virtuous cycle of support and momentum for your ongoing efforts.

Chapter 9
Maintaining Work-Life Balance and Avoiding Burnout

Setting Realistic Goals and Boundaries

Hey there, you hard-working online business dynamo! I know you're probably feeling pretty pumped up and inspired after reading all those amazing success stories and case studies in the last chapter. And I don't blame you – it's easy to get caught up in the excitement and possibility of entrepreneurship, and want to go all-in on your business 24/7.

But here's the thing – as important as it is to hustle and chase your dreams, it's equally important (if not more so) to take care of yourself and maintain a healthy work-life balance along the way. Because let's face it – burnout is real, and it's not pretty.

When you're running your own online business, it's easy to blur the lines between work and life, and feel like you need to be "on" all the time. After all, there's always more to do, more to learn, and more to achieve, right? But if you're not careful, that constant pressure and stress can quickly lead to exhaustion, overwhelm, and even resentment towards your business.

And trust me, that's not a recipe for long-term success or happiness. In fact, it's a surefire way to kill your creativity, productivity, and passion for your work – not to mention your relationships, health, and overall well-being.

So how do you avoid falling into the trap of burnout and maintain a healthy work-life balance as an online business owner? It all starts with setting realistic goals and boundaries for yourself and your business.

Let's dive in and explore some practical strategies and mindset shifts you can use to set yourself up for sustainable success and satisfaction in both your work and your life.

1. Define Your Priorities and Values
The first step in setting realistic goals and boundaries for your business is to get clear on your priorities and values – both in work and in life.

Take some time to reflect on what truly matters most to you, and what kind of lifestyle and impact you want to create through your business. Ask yourself questions like:

- What are my non-negotiable personal values and needs (e.g. health, family, creativity, freedom)?
- What are my top business goals and milestones, and why are they important to me?
- What does success and fulfillment look like for me, both personally and professionally?
- How much time, energy, and resources am I realistically willing and able to invest in my business?
- Be honest with yourself about your capacity, constraints, and desires – and use that self-awareness to inform your goal-setting and boundary-setting process.
- Remember, your business should support and enhance your life – not consume or diminish it. So make sure your goals and priorities are aligned with your overall vision and values.

2. Set SMART Goals and Milestones

Once you've clarified your priorities and values, it's time to translate them into specific, measurable, achievable, relevant, and time-bound (SMART) goals and milestones for your business.

Break down your big-picture vision into smaller, actionable steps and targets that you can work towards on a daily, weekly, and monthly basis. For example:

- Instead of setting a vague goal like "grow my email list", set a SMART goal like "add 500 new email subscribers per month through targeted lead magnets and social media campaigns".
- Instead of trying to do everything at once, focus on 1-3 key priorities or projects at a time, and set realistic deadlines and milestones for each one.
- Instead of comparing yourself to others or chasing vanity metrics, define what success and progress look like for YOU and your business, and celebrate your wins along the way.
- Be realistic and honest with yourself about what you can achieve given your current resources, skills, and bandwidth – and be willing to adjust your goals and expectations as needed.
- Use tools like project management software, calendars, and accountability partners to help you stay organized, focused, and on track with your goals and milestones.

3. Establish Clear Boundaries and Non-Negotiables

In addition to setting realistic goals, it's equally important to establish clear boundaries and non-negotiables around your time, energy, and workflow as an online business owner.

Define what your ideal work schedule and environment look like, and communicate those boundaries to your clients, partners, and team members. For example:

- Set specific work hours and stick to them as much as possible (e.g. 9am-5pm on weekdays, no work on weekends).
- Create a dedicated workspace that is separate from your personal living areas, and minimize distractions and interruptions during your work time.
- Communicate your availability and response times to clients and collaborators, and set expectations around project timelines and deliverables.
- Identify your personal non-negotiables and self-care practices, and make them a non-negotiable part of your daily or weekly routine. For example:
- Taking regular breaks and time off to rest, recharge, and pursue hobbies and interests outside of work.
- Prioritizing sleep, nutrition, exercise, and stress management practices that keep you healthy and energized.
- Spending quality time with loved ones and maintaining social connections and support systems.
- Learn to say no to projects, opportunities, or requests that don't align with your goals, values, or boundaries – and trust that the right things will come to you at the right time.

Remember, your time and energy are your most valuable resources as an entrepreneur – so be intentional and proactive about protecting and investing them wisely.

4. Delegate and Automate Where Possible

Another key strategy for maintaining work-life balance and avoiding burnout is to delegate and automate as much as possible in your business.

Identify tasks or areas of your business that you can outsource to freelancers, contractors, or virtual assistants – especially those that are time-consuming, repetitive, or outside of your zone of genius. For example:

- Administrative tasks like email management, scheduling, or data entry
- Technical tasks like website maintenance, graphic design, or video editing
- Marketing tasks like social media management, content creation, or paid advertising
- Invest in tools and systems that can automate and streamline your workflows and processes, such as:
- Email marketing platforms that allow you to create and schedule automated email sequences and campaigns
- Social media scheduling tools that allow you to batch and schedule your content in advance
- Project management and collaboration tools that help you track and organize your tasks and communications

By delegating and automating the tasks that drain your time and energy, you free up more space and bandwidth to focus on the high-impact, high-value activities that truly move the needle in your business and life.

Plus, you create opportunities for others to contribute their skills and expertise to your vision, and build a more scalable and sustainable business in the process.

5. Practice Self-Compassion and Gratitude

Finally, one of the most important mindset shifts you can make to maintain work-life balance and avoid burnout is to practice self-compassion and gratitude on a daily basis.

Recognize that entrepreneurship is a marathon, not a sprint – and that there will be ups and downs, successes and failures, and lessons learned along the way. Be kind and patient with yourself as you navigate the journey.

Celebrate your progress and victories, no matter how small – and reframe challenges and setbacks as opportunities for growth and resilience. Focus on how far you've come, not just how far you have to go.

Cultivate an attitude of gratitude for the privilege and opportunity to pursue your passions and make a difference through your business – and for all the people and resources that support you along the way.

Make time for reflection, introspection, and self-care practices that help you stay grounded, centered, and connected to your purpose and values. Whether it's journaling, meditation, nature walks, or creative hobbies – find what works for you and make it a non-negotiable part of your routine.

Remember, your business is not your identity or your worth – it's just one expression of your gifts and talents in the world. Don't let it consume or define you – let it enrich and inspire you, and trust that your value and potential extend far beyond your professional achievements.

Setting realistic goals and boundaries, delegating and automating where possible, and practicing self-compassion and gratitude – these are the keys to maintaining a healthy and sustainable work-life balance as an online business owner.

It's not always easy, and it takes ongoing effort and intention – but it's so worth it. Because when you take care of yourself first, you show up as the best version of yourself in your business and your life. You have more energy, creativity, and resilience to weather the ups and downs of entrepreneurship, and to create the impact and lifestyle you truly desire.

So give yourself permission to prioritize your well-being, set realistic expectations, and enjoy the journey – not just the destination. Your business, your loved ones, and the world will thank you for it.

And there you have it – a deep dive into the art and science of maintaining work-life balance and avoiding burnout as an online business owner. I hope this chapter has given you some practical strategies and mindset shifts to help you set realistic goals and boundaries, delegate and automate where possible, and practice self-compassion and gratitude along the way. Remember – you are the most valuable asset in your business, so take care of yourself first and trust that everything else will fall into place. You've got this!

Prioritizing Self-Care and Mental Health

Hey there, you amazing human being! Can we take a moment to talk about something really important? I know you're probably super busy building your online business, chasing your dreams, and trying to make a difference in the world – and that's awesome! But there's something else that's just as important (if not more so) than all of those external goals and achievements. And that's taking care of yourself and your mental health.

I know, I know – self-care and mental health can sometimes feel like buzzwords or low priorities when you're in the thick of entrepreneurship. There's always more to do, more to learn, and more to prove – and it can be easy to put your own needs on the back burner in pursuit of success.

But here's the thing – neglecting your self-care and mental health is like trying to run a marathon without any food, water, or rest. Sure, you might be able to push through for a little while on sheer adrenaline and willpower – but eventually, you'll hit a wall. And that wall can look like burnout, anxiety, depression, physical illness, or worse.

The truth is, your mental health is the foundation of everything else in your life and business. It's what allows you to show up with clarity, creativity, resilience, and compassion – both for yourself and for others. It's what fuels your passion, purpose, and productivity – and it's what sustains you through the inevitable ups and downs of entrepreneurship.

So if you want to build a truly successful and fulfilling online business (and life), prioritizing your self-care and mental health needs to be non-negotiable. It's not a sign of weakness or indulgence – it's a sign of strength and wisdom.

But what does that actually look like in practice? How can you make self-care and mental health a priority when you've got a million things on your plate and a never-ending to-do list?
Here are some practical strategies and mindset shifts to help you prioritize your well-being and build a more sustainable, joyful, and impactful business and life:

1. Redefine Success and Productivity
One of the biggest obstacles to prioritizing self-care and mental health is the pressure to constantly be productive, successful, and "on" as an entrepreneur. We live in a culture that glorifies hustle, grind, and achievement above all else – and it can be easy to internalize those messages and feel like you're never doing enough.

But here's the thing – true success and productivity aren't just about how much you do or how fast you grow your business. They're about how well you show up for yourself and others, how aligned you are with your values and purpose, and how much joy and fulfillment you experience along the way.

So take some time to redefine what success and productivity mean to you – beyond just the external metrics and milestones. What does a truly successful and productive day, week, or month look like for you? How do you want to feel in your business and your life? What really matters most to you?

Then, start aligning your goals, habits, and routines with those definitions – and give yourself permission to focus on the things that truly nourish and energize you, even if they don't always look "productive" on paper. Whether it's taking a nap, going for a walk in nature, or spending quality time with loved ones – those activities are just as important (if not more so) than crushing your to-do list or hitting your revenue goals.

2. Set Boundaries and Non-Negotiables

Another key to prioritizing self-care and mental health is setting clear boundaries and non-negotiables around your time, energy, and attention. As an online business owner, it can be tempting to say yes to every opportunity, request, or demand that comes your way – but that's a surefire recipe for overwhelm and burnout.

So take some time to identify your personal and professional boundaries – the things that you need to feel healthy, happy, and whole in your business and your life. Maybe it's a certain number of hours you're willing to work each day, or a certain type of client or project you're not willing to take on. Maybe it's a daily self-care practice that you commit to no matter what, or a regular day off that you protect fiercely.

Then, communicate those boundaries clearly and consistently to your clients, partners, and team members – and hold yourself accountable to honoring them, even when it's uncomfortable or inconvenient. Remember, your boundaries are not a sign of selfishness or weakness – they're a sign of self-respect and self-preservation.

And when you do need to be flexible or make exceptions, make sure you're doing it consciously and intentionally – not just out of guilt, fear, or people-pleasing. Ask yourself: "Is this aligned with my values and priorities? Is it worth the trade-off in terms of my well-being and balance?" If not, it's okay to say no or find another way.

3. Create a Supportive Environment and Network

As an online business owner, it's easy to feel isolated, overwhelmed, and like you have to do everything on your own. But the truth is, we all need support, connection, and community to thrive – both personally and professionally.

So make it a priority to surround yourself with people, places, and things that uplift and inspire you – and that make you feel seen, heard, and valued for who you are, not just what you do. Whether it's a mastermind group of fellow entrepreneurs, a trusted coach or mentor, or a circle of friends who get what you're going through – find your people and lean on them regularly.

Create a physical environment that feels nourishing and energizing to you – whether it's a cozy home office, a vibrant co-working space, or a peaceful spot in nature. Fill it with things that bring you joy, inspiration, and comfort – like plants, artwork, photos, or affirmations.

And don't be afraid to ask for help or delegate when you need it – whether it's hiring a virtual assistant, outsourcing a project, or simply reaching out to a friend or family member for support. Remember, you don't have to do it all alone – and there's strength and wisdom in knowing when to ask for help.

4. Prioritize Rest and Recovery

In a culture that's obsessed with hustle and productivity, rest and recovery can often feel like a luxury or an afterthought. But the truth is, they're essential for our physical, mental, and emotional well-being – and they're just as important (if not more so) than the work itself.

So make rest and recovery a non-negotiable part of your daily and weekly routine – whether it's getting enough sleep, taking regular breaks throughout the day, or scheduling in full days off to unplug and recharge. Treat it like an important meeting or deadline – because it is!

Experiment with different self-care practices and find what works best for you – whether it's meditation, yoga, exercise, journaling, or creative hobbies. The key is to find activities that help you feel grounded, centered, and connected to yourself and your needs.

And remember, rest and recovery don't always have to mean doing nothing – they can also mean engaging in activities that energize and inspire you, like learning something new, connecting with loved ones, or giving back to your community. The goal is to fill your cup in whatever way feels most nourishing and restorative to you.

5. Practice Self-Compassion and Gratitude

Finally, one of the most powerful ways to prioritize your self-care and mental health is to practice self-compassion and gratitude on a daily basis. As entrepreneurs, we're often our own worst critics – holding ourselves to impossible standards, beating ourselves up for every mistake or setback, and comparing ourselves to others who seem to have it all together.

But here's the thing – that kind of self-judgment and negativity is not only unhelpful, but it's actually harmful to our well-being and success. It zaps our energy, creativity, and motivation – and it keeps us stuck in a cycle of stress and self-doubt.

So instead, try practicing self-compassion – treating yourself with the same kindness, understanding, and forgiveness that you would offer to a good friend. Acknowledge that you're doing the best you can with what you have, and that every challenge is an opportunity for growth and learning.

And make it a daily habit to focus on gratitude – taking time to appreciate and savor the good things in your life, no matter how small. Whether it's a beautiful sunrise, a kind words from a friend, or a small win in your business – train your brain to look for the positive and the beautiful, even in the midst of struggle or uncertainty.

Remember, your thoughts and beliefs have a powerful impact on your mental health and well-being – so choose them wisely. Surround yourself with affirmations, inspirations, and reminders of your worth and potential – and let them be your anchor when the waves of self-doubt or stress come crashing in.

Prioritizing self-care and mental health as an online business owner is not always easy – but it's always worth it. It's an ongoing practice and commitment – one that requires patience, compassion, and a willingness to put yourself first, even when it feels selfish or scary.

But here's the beautiful truth: when you take care of yourself first, you become a better entrepreneur, leader, and human being. You have more to give – to your business, your loved ones, and the world. You show up with more clarity, creativity, and resilience – and you inspire others to do the same.

So make self-care and mental health a non-negotiable part of your entrepreneurial journey – not just for your own sake, but for the sake of the impact and legacy you want to create. Trust that when you put your well-being first, everything else will fall into place – and you'll be able to build a business and life that truly lights you up, inside and out.

You've got this, my friend. Take a deep breath, put your hand on your heart, and remember: you are worthy, you are enough, and you are so deeply loved.

And there you have it – a heartfelt and practical guide to prioritizing self-care and mental health as an online business owner. I hope this chapter has given you some valuable strategies, perspectives, and reminders to help you put yourself first and build a more sustainable, joyful, and impactful business and life. Remember – you are the most important asset in your business, and your well-being is the foundation of everything else. So take care of yourself, be kind to yourself, and trust that the rest will follow. You've got this!

Automating and Streamlining Your Business Processes

Hey there, you savvy online business owner! Are you ready to take your productivity and efficiency to the next level? Because let me tell you, one of the most powerful ways to grow your business and free up your time and energy is to automate and streamline your processes.

I know, I know – as entrepreneurs, we often pride ourselves on being able to do it all, wear all the hats, and juggle all the balls. But here's the thing – just because you can do something, doesn't mean you should.

The truth is, trying to manually handle every task and process in your business is not only time-consuming and stressful – it's also not the most effective use of your unique skills and talents. As the visionary and leader of your business, your time and energy are best spent on the high-level, high-impact activities that only you can do – like strategizing, creating, and building relationships.

But when you're bogged down in the day-to-day minutiae of running your business – like sending emails, scheduling appointments, or managing social media – you're not only limiting your own potential, but you're also limiting the potential of your business to grow and scale.

That's where automation and streamlining come in – by using tools, systems, and processes to handle the repetitive, time-consuming tasks in your business, you can free up your time and energy to focus on the things that truly move the needle and light you up.

So how can you start automating and streamlining your business processes? Here are some practical strategies and tools to get you started:

1. Identify Your Most Time-Consuming and Repetitive Tasks

The first step in automating and streamlining your business processes is to take inventory of all the tasks and activities that you currently handle on a daily, weekly, or monthly basis. Make a list of everything you do – from checking and responding to emails, to scheduling social media posts, to invoicing clients and tracking expenses.

Then, identify the tasks that take up the most time, energy, or mental bandwidth – the ones that feel repetitive, tedious, or draining. These are the prime candidates for automation and streamlining.

Also, consider the tasks that are prone to human error or inconsistency – like data entry, calculations, or communication. These are areas where automation can not only save you time, but also improve the accuracy and quality of your work.

2. Research and Invest in Automation Tools and Software

Once you've identified the tasks and processes that you want to automate, it's time to research and invest in the tools and software that can help you do it. There are countless options out there – from all-in-one business management platforms, to specific tools for email marketing, social media scheduling, or financial tracking.

Some popular automation tools and software for online businesses include:

- Zapier: A tool that allows you to connect and automate tasks between different apps and platforms (like sending new leads from your website to your email marketing software).
- Hootsuite or Buffer: Social media scheduling and management tools that allow you to plan, create, and publish content across multiple platforms.
- Mailchimp or ConvertKit: Email marketing platforms that allow you to create, send, and track automated email campaigns and sequences.
- Quickbooks or Xero: Financial management and accounting software that allows you to automate invoicing, expense tracking, and tax reporting.

When choosing automation tools and software, consider factors like ease of use, integrations with other tools you use, pricing and scalability, and customer support and reviews. And don't be afraid to invest in the tools that will truly save you time and energy in the long run – they'll pay for themselves many times over!

3. Create Standard Operating Procedures (SOPs) and Templates

Another key way to streamline your business processes is to create standard operating procedures (SOPs) and templates for the tasks and activities that you do regularly. SOPs are step-by-step instructions or checklists that outline exactly how to complete a specific task or process – from start to finish.

By documenting your SOPs and creating templates for things like email responses, social media posts, or client onboarding, you can save time and ensure consistency and quality in your work. Instead of having to recreate the wheel every time you do a task, you can simply follow the SOP or use the template as a starting point.

Some tips for creating effective SOPs and templates:

- Break down each task or process into clear, specific steps that anyone could follow (even if they're not familiar with your business).
- Use visuals, screenshots, or videos to illustrate each step and make the instructions easy to follow.
- Include any necessary links, login information, or resources needed to complete the task.
- Store your SOPs and templates in a centralized, easily accessible place (like Google Drive or Dropbox) and make sure your team members have access to them.

By creating SOPs and templates, you not only streamline your own workflows, but you also make it easier to delegate or outsource tasks to team members or contractors in the future.

4. Automate Your Client and Customer Communication

One of the most time-consuming aspects of running an online business is communicating with clients and customers – whether it's responding to inquiries, sending welcome packets, or following up after a sale. But with automation tools and templates, you can streamline your communication and provide a better experience for your clients and customers.

Some ways to automate your client and customer communication:
- Use email marketing software (like Mailchimp or ConvertKit) to create automated welcome sequences, nurture campaigns, or post-purchase follow-ups.
- Use chatbots or auto-responders on your website or social media to answer common questions or direct people to helpful resources.
- Create templates for common email responses (like inquiries, onboarding, or offboarding) and use a tool like TextExpander or Canned Responses to insert them with a quick shortcut.
- Use a scheduling tool (like Calendly or Acuity) to allow clients and customers to book appointments or consultations with you automatically.

By automating your communication, you can save time, improve your response times, and provide a more professional and consistent experience for your clients and customers.

5. Continuously Evaluate and Optimize Your Processes

Finally, it's important to remember that automating and streamlining your business processes is not a one-time event – it's an ongoing practice of evaluation and optimization. As your business grows and evolves, so too will your tasks, tools, and workflows.

Make it a habit to regularly review your processes and look for opportunities to automate, streamline, or improve them. Ask yourself:
- What tasks or processes are still taking up too much time or energy?

- What tools or systems are working well, and which ones need to be updated or replaced?
- What feedback or suggestions do my team members or clients have for improving our processes?
- What new tools, technologies, or best practices could we implement to work smarter and more efficiently?

Be open to experimentation and iteration – try out new tools or approaches, measure their impact, and be willing to pivot or adjust as needed. And don't be afraid to invest in training, coaching, or resources to help you continuously improve and optimize your business processes.

Automating and streamlining your business processes is not about sacrificing quality or personal touch – it's about leveraging technology and systems to create more space and capacity for the things that truly matter. When you automate the repetitive, time-consuming tasks in your business, you free up your time and energy to focus on the high-impact, meaningful work that only you can do.

And the benefits go beyond just saving time and increasing efficiency – by streamlining your processes, you also create a more professional, consistent, and scalable business that can grow and evolve with you over time. You'll be able to take on more clients, projects, or opportunities without sacrificing your sanity or your standards.

So if you're ready to take your online business to the next level of productivity and profitability, start by identifying the tasks and processes that are holding you back – and then invest in the tools, systems, and strategies to automate and streamline them.

Your future self (and your bottom line) will thank you!

And there you have it – a comprehensive guide to automating and streamlining your business processes as an online entrepreneur. I hope this chapter has given you some practical ideas, tools, and frameworks to help you work smarter, not harder – and create more time, energy, and space for the things that truly light you up. Remember, your business should support your life, not consume it – so don't be afraid to automate, delegate, and simplify wherever you can. You've got this!

The Importance of Continuous Learning and Personal Development

Hey there, you lifelong learner and growth-seeker! Can I just take a moment to celebrate you and your commitment to continuous learning and personal development? Because in today's fast-paced, ever-changing world, the ability to learn, grow, and adapt is not just a nice-to-have – it's a must-have for success and fulfillment, both in business and in life.

But what exactly do we mean by continuous learning and personal development? And why is it so important, especially for online business owners and entrepreneurs?

At its core, continuous learning is about maintaining a growth mindset – a belief that your abilities, skills, and knowledge are not fixed, but can be developed and expanded through effort, experience, and education. It's about embracing curiosity, seeking out new ideas and perspectives, and being willing to step outside your comfort zone to try new things and take on new challenges.

Personal development, on the other hand, is about intentionally working on yourself – your mindset, habits, behaviors, and skills – to become the best version of yourself. It's about identifying your strengths and weaknesses, setting goals and intentions, and taking consistent action to grow and improve in all areas of your life – from your health and relationships, to your career and finances.

Together, continuous learning and personal development create a powerful combination – a virtuous cycle of growth and improvement that can transform your life and business in incredible ways.

But why is this so important for online business owners and entrepreneurs specifically? Here are just a few key reasons:

1. The Online Business Landscape is Constantly Changing

If there's one thing that's constant in the world of online business, it's change. New technologies, platforms, strategies, and best practices are emerging all the time – and what worked yesterday may not work tomorrow.

To stay competitive and relevant in your industry, you need to be constantly learning and adapting to these changes. Whether it's keeping up with the latest social media trends, mastering new marketing techniques, or developing new products or services to meet evolving customer needs – the ability to learn and pivot quickly is essential for long-term success.

2. Your Personal Growth Directly Impacts Your Business Growth

As an online business owner, your business is a direct reflection of you – your skills, knowledge, mindset, and habits. The more you grow and develop as a person, the more your business will grow and thrive as a result.

Think about it – if you're constantly learning new skills and strategies, you'll be able to offer more value to your clients and customers. If you're working on your mindset and resilience, you'll be better equipped to handle the challenges and setbacks of entrepreneurship.

If you're developing your leadership and communication skills, you'll be able to build stronger relationships and teams to support your vision.

Your personal development is not separate from your business development – it's the foundation of it. By investing in yourself, you're also investing in the future of your business.

3. Continuous Learning Helps You Stay Inspired and Motivated

Let's be real – running an online business can be tough, lonely, and overwhelming at times. It's easy to get stuck in a rut, lose motivation, or feel like you're not making progress fast enough.

But when you make continuous learning and personal development a priority, you're giving yourself a constant source of inspiration, motivation, and renewed energy. Every new skill you learn, every book you read, every course you take, every person you meet – they all have the potential to spark new ideas, insights, and opportunities for your business.

By staying curious and engaged in the world around you, you're feeding your mind and soul with the fuel it needs to keep going, even when things get tough. You're reminding yourself of the bigger picture – the impact and legacy you want to create through your work.

4. Personal Development Helps You Overcome Limiting Beliefs and Fears

As an entrepreneur, your mindset is everything. Your beliefs, thoughts, and fears can either propel you forward or hold you back from reaching your full potential.

But through personal development practices like mindfulness, therapy, coaching, or self-reflection, you can identify and overcome the limiting beliefs and fears that are holding you back. Whether it's imposter syndrome, fear of failure, or self-doubt – by working on your inner game, you can develop the confidence, resilience, and self-awareness to push through these barriers and take bold action towards your goals.

Remember – your business can only grow to the extent that you do. By investing in your own personal growth and development, you're breaking through the mental and emotional blocks that are keeping you stuck, and creating space for new levels of success and fulfillment.

5. Continuous Learning Helps You Innovate and Stand Out in Your Industry

In today's crowded and noisy online marketplace, it's not enough to just be good at what you do – you need to be different, better, and more valuable than your competitors.

But how do you stand out and innovate in your industry? By continuously learning and exploring new ideas, perspectives, and approaches. By seeking out diverse knowledge and experiences that broaden your horizons and challenge your assumptions. By staying curious and open to new possibilities, even if they seem unconventional or risky.

When you make continuous learning a habit, you're not just acquiring new knowledge – you're developing your creativity, critical thinking, and problem-solving skills. You're training your brain to see opportunities and connections that others might miss. You're becoming a thought leader and innovator in your field.

So, how can you make continuous learning and personal development a priority in your life and business? Here are a few practical tips and strategies:

1. Set Learning Goals and Create a Personal Development Plan

Just like you set goals and create plans for your business, do the same for your personal growth and development. Identify the skills, knowledge, and areas of growth that are most important to you and your business, and create a plan to pursue them intentionally.

This could include things like:
- Taking an online course or workshop to learn a new skill or strategy
- Reading books or articles on topics related to your industry or personal development
- Attending conferences, meetups, or networking events to connect with others and learn from their experiences
- Working with a coach, mentor, or accountability partner to stay motivated and on track
- Setting aside dedicated time each week for learning and reflection

By creating a clear plan and structure for your learning and development, you're more likely to follow through and make consistent progress over time.

2. Embrace a Growth Mindset and Celebrate Your Progress

Remember, continuous learning and personal development is not about achieving perfection or reaching a finish line – it's about embracing the journey of growth and improvement.

Cultivate a growth mindset by reframing challenges and setbacks as opportunities to learn and grow. Celebrate your progress and milestones along the way, no matter how small. Recognize that every step you take towards your goals is a step in the right direction.

And don't compare your journey to anyone else's – focus on your own path and progress. Everyone's learning and development journey is unique, and there's no one-size-fits-all approach. Trust your own timing and process.

3. Seek Out Diverse Perspectives and Experiences

One of the best ways to accelerate your learning and personal growth is to seek out diverse perspectives and experiences that challenge your assumptions and expand your horizons.

This could include things like:
- Reading books or articles from authors with different backgrounds, cultures, or viewpoints than your own
- Following and engaging with thought leaders and influencers in industries outside of your own
- Traveling to new places or immersing yourself in different cultures and communities
- Collaborating with people who have different skills, strengths, or approaches than you
- Trying new hobbies, activities, or experiences that push you outside your comfort zone

By exposing yourself to diverse ideas and experiences, you're not only learning new things – you're also developing your empathy, adaptability, and creativity. You're becoming a more well-rounded and open-minded person and entrepreneur.

4. Prioritize Rest, Reflection, and Self-Care

While continuous learning and personal development are important, it's equally important to prioritize rest, reflection, and self-care in the process. Your brain and body need downtime to integrate new information, recharge, and avoid burnout.

Make sure to schedule regular breaks and time off to rest and recharge. Take time to reflect on your learning and experiences, and how you can apply them to your life and business. Practice self-care activities that nourish your mind, body, and spirit – whether it's meditation, exercise, time in nature, or creative hobbies.

Remember, continuous learning and personal development is a marathon, not a sprint. It's important to pace yourself, listen to your needs, and prioritize your well-being along the way.

5. Share Your Learning and Insights with Others

Finally, one of the best ways to reinforce your own learning and development is to share your insights and knowledge with others. When you teach or share what you've learned, you not only help others grow – you also deepen your own understanding and retention of the material.

- Look for opportunities to share your learning and insights with your audience, clients, peers, or team members. This could include things like:
  - Writing blog posts or articles about your key takeaways and insights from a course or book
  - Creating social media posts or videos sharing tips, strategies, or lessons learned
  - Leading workshops, webinars, or trainings on topics related to your area of expertise
  - Mentoring or coaching others who are earlier in their learning and development journey
  - Participating in mastermind groups or online communities to share ideas and support each other's growth

By sharing your learning and insights with others, you're not only reinforcing your own knowledge – you're also positioning yourself as a thought leader and expert in your field. You're building your brand and reputation as someone who is constantly growing, evolving, and adding value to others.

Continuous learning and personal development is not a luxury or a nice-to-have – it's a necessity for anyone who wants to thrive and make a meaningful impact in today's world, especially as an online business owner and entrepreneur. It's the key to staying relevant, competitive, and fulfilled in your work and life.

But more than that, it's a mindset and a lifestyle – a commitment to always be growing, evolving, and becoming the best version of yourself. It's a journey of self-discovery, self-mastery, and self-actualization that has no end point or destination.

So embrace the journey of continuous learning and personal development, and trust that every step you take is leading you closer to your highest potential and purpose. Your future self (and the world) will thank you for it!

And there you have it – a deep dive into the importance of continuous learning and personal development for online business owners and entrepreneurs. I hope this chapter has inspired you to make learning and growth a lifelong priority, and given you some practical strategies and mindset shifts to help you on your journey. Remember – your business can only grow to the extent that you do. So keep learning, keep growing, and keep shining your light. The best is yet to come!

Conclusion

Recap of Key Takeaways and Action Steps

Wow, what a journey it's been! Throughout this book, we've explored the ins and outs of starting and growing a profitable online business – from choosing your niche and building your website, to creating compelling content and products, to marketing and scaling your business through various strategies and channels.

We've covered a lot of ground and delved into many different aspects of online entrepreneurship. But if there are a few key takeaways and action steps that I hope you'll remember and implement, they are these:

1. Clarity is key. Take the time to get clear on your unique strengths, passions, and purpose, and use that clarity to guide your niche selection, branding, and content creation. The more specific and authentic you can be in your business, the more you'll attract and resonate with your ideal audience.

2. Consistency is queen. Whether it's publishing blog posts, sending email newsletters, or showing up on social media, consistency is essential for building trust, authority, and momentum in your online business. Create a realistic content calendar and stick to it, even when motivation wanes.

3. Relationships are everything. Online business is not just about transactions and algorithms – it's about real human connections and relationships. Focus on serving your audience with genuine value and care, and look for

opportunities to collaborate and partner with others in your industry. Your network is your net worth.

4. Experimentation is essential. The online world is always evolving, and what works today may not work tomorrow. Embrace a spirit of experimentation and be willing to try new things, test different strategies, and pivot when necessary. The most successful online businesses are the ones that stay agile and adaptable.

5. Mindset is the foundation. More than any tactic or tool, your mindset is the most important factor in your online business success. Work on cultivating a growth mindset, resilience, and self-belief, and surround yourself with supportive people and resources. Your business can only grow to the extent that you do.

The Future of Online Business and Emerging Trends

As we look to the future of online business, one thing is certain: change is the only constant. New technologies, platforms, and consumer behaviors are emerging all the time, and what worked yesterday may not work tomorrow.

Some of the key trends and opportunities that I see shaping the future of online business include:

1. The rise of AI and automation. From chatbots and personalized recommendations to content creation and customer service, artificial intelligence and automation are transforming the way online businesses operate and interact with customers. As these technologies become more sophisticated and accessible, they'll open up new possibilities for efficiency, personalization, and innovation.

2. The growing importance of video and interactive content. As attention spans shrink and screens multiply, video and interactive content are becoming increasingly essential for engaging and converting online audiences. From live streaming and stories to webinars and online courses, businesses that can create compelling, multi-sensory experiences will stand out and thrive.

3. The emergence of voice search and virtual assistants. With the proliferation of smart speakers and virtual assistants like Siri and Alexa, voice search is becoming a more common way for people to find and interact with online businesses. Optimizing your content and offerings for voice search and conversational interfaces will be key to staying visible and relevant in the years ahead.

4. The shift towards niche communities and micro-influencers. As social media algorithms prioritize engagement over reach, and consumers crave more authentic and specialized experiences, niche communities and micro-influencers are becoming more valuable than broad, mass-market approaches. Building and nurturing engaged, loyal communities around specific interests and identities will be essential for online business growth and sustainability.

5. The increasing demand for purpose-driven and socially responsible business. As consumers become more conscious and values-driven in their purchasing decisions, online businesses that demonstrate a genuine commitment to social and environmental responsibility will have a competitive advantage.

From eco-friendly products and packaging to ethical supply chains and giving back programs, aligning your business with a larger purpose and positive impact will be key to attracting and retaining customers.

Of course, these are just a few of the many trends and possibilities shaping the future of online business. The key is to stay informed, adaptable, and open to new opportunities as they arise, while staying true to your core values and vision.

Encouragement and Motivation for the Reader's Journey Ahead

As we come to the end of this book, I want to leave you with a few words of encouragement and motivation for your online business journey ahead.

Building and growing a successful online business is not a quick or easy path. It takes time, effort, persistence, and a willingness to face challenges and setbacks along the way. There will be moments of doubt, frustration, and overwhelm – but there will also be moments of joy, pride, and fulfillment that make it all worthwhile.

Remember that every successful online entrepreneur started where you are now – with an idea, a passion, and a willingness to take action and learn as they go. They faced fears, made mistakes, and pivoted many times along the way. But they kept going, kept growing, and kept believing in their vision and their ability to make it a reality.

So as you embark on your own online business journey, I encourage you to:

1. Start where you are, with what you have. Don't wait for perfect conditions or resources to get started. Take small, consistent steps every day towards your goals, and trust that progress will compound over time.

2. Embrace the journey, not just the destination. Building an online business is not a linear or predictable path. Enjoy the process of learning, creating, and connecting with others along the way, and celebrate your progress and milestones, no matter how small.

3. Surround yourself with support and inspiration. Building an online business can be lonely and challenging at times. Seek out mentors, peers, and communities that can offer guidance, encouragement, and accountability along the way. Feed your mind and soul with books, podcasts, and experiences that inspire and motivate you to keep going.

4. Trust your unique voice and value. In a crowded and noisy online world, it can be tempting to compare yourself to others or try to fit in with the crowd. But your greatest asset is your authenticity and your unique perspective and experiences. Don't be afraid to stand out, speak up, and share your gifts with the world.

5. Remember your why and your impact. When the going gets tough, remember why you started your online business in the first place – the passion, the purpose, the difference you want to make in people's lives. Keep your vision and your values at the forefront of everything you do, and trust that your work is making a positive ripple effect in the world, even if you can't always see it.

Building an online business is not just about making money or achieving fame – it's about creating a life and a legacy that aligns with your deepest values and desires. It's about taking control of your time, your energy, and your impact, and using your gifts to make a difference in the world.

So as you continue on your online business journey, remember that you are capable, worthy, and destined for great things. You have a unique story, perspective, and purpose that the world needs to hear and benefit from.

Keep learning, keep growing, and keep showing up with authenticity, generosity, and resilience. The universe is conspiring in your favor, and your dreams are closer than you think.

Believe in yourself, take inspired action, and trust the journey. Your online business success story is just beginning, and I can't wait to see where it takes you!

And with that, we come to the end of our journey through the world of online business and entrepreneurship. Thank you for joining me on this adventure of learning, growth, and possibility. I hope that the strategies, insights, and stories shared in this book have inspired and empowered you to turn your passions and skills into a thriving online business that supports your dreams and makes a difference in the world.

Remember, success is not a destination, but a journey of continuous learning, experimentation, and self-discovery. Embrace the ups and downs, the challenges and the triumphs, and trust that every step is leading you closer to your highest potential and purpose.

You have everything you need within you to create the business and life you truly desire. So keep shining your light, keep following your heart, and keep believing in the power of your dreams. The world is waiting for your unique gifts and contributions.

*Thank you for being a part of this community of passionate, purposeful, and unstoppable online entrepreneurs. I believe in you, and I'm cheering you on every step of the way!

Here's to your success, your happiness, and your impact. May your online business be a source of joy, abundance, and fulfillment for you and all those you serve.

*With gratitude and excitement for your journey ahead,

www.ingramcontent.com/pod-product-compliance
Lightning Source LLC
Chambersburg PA
CBHW071206240526
45470CB00018B/1516